Designed for You

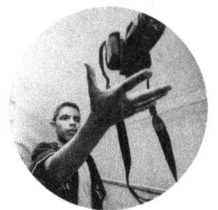

I0492226

You,

who are a photographer and who multiply the ideas of photoshoots and photos not to be forgotten.

You, who have a great need for organization to achieve them, this photoshoot planner & log book has been specially designed for you.

From the definition of your project to the publication of your photos, this log book will allow you to shape your ideas, organize your shootings and finally produce the images of your dreams.

Technical settings, moodboard, monthly schedules, shooting files, an essential shooting notebook to stay focused on the essentials and soon publish your photos.

Let's make room for creativity and the realization of your dreams.

A professional photographer,
who has for a long time lost her inspiration, and who tries every day to improve with the support of this log book!

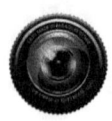

This Photoshoot log book

Belongs to

SURNAME/ NAME

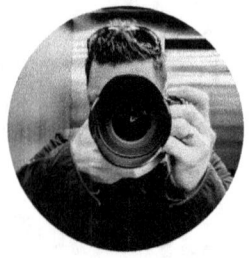

ADDRESS

MAIL

PHONE

WEBSITE

SOCIAL NETWORKS

MY GOAL IS:

Ultimate Photoshoot Logbook

CONTENT

TECHNICAL SETTINGS
101: the basics

MY SETTINGS
Settings already tested to not forget

MY EQUIPMENT
All your must have equipments listed here to be ready before your photo shooting

CREATIVE IDEAS
53 themes to remain inspired all along the year

MONTHLY PLANNING
Month by month, define your photo goal and the associated actions

MIND MAP
List all the steps to create amazing pictures

MY PHOTO SHOOTING SHEETS

Summary of shooting sheets (up to 15 shootings)

For each shooting sheet, 7 pages to shape your ideas and organize your shooting session around the following themes:
- Goal
- Moodboard
- Dedicated Team
- Styling
- Decoration
- Technical settings (camera, light,...)
- Equipment
- Photo editing

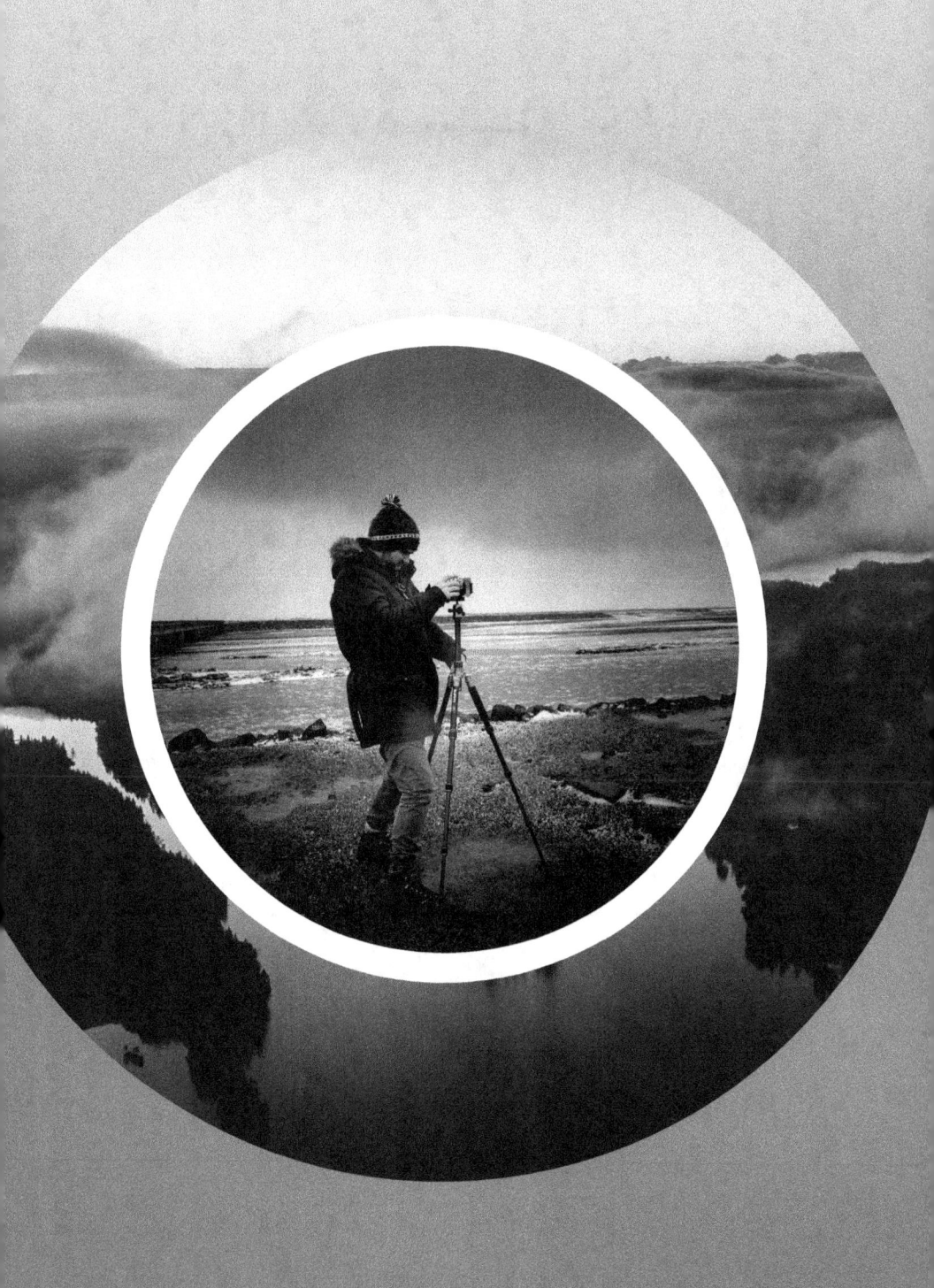

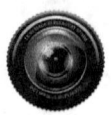

Technical settings

Reminder

◉ F22   ◉ F16   ○ F11

○ F8   ○ F5.6   ○ F4

○ F2.8   ○ F2   ○ F1.4

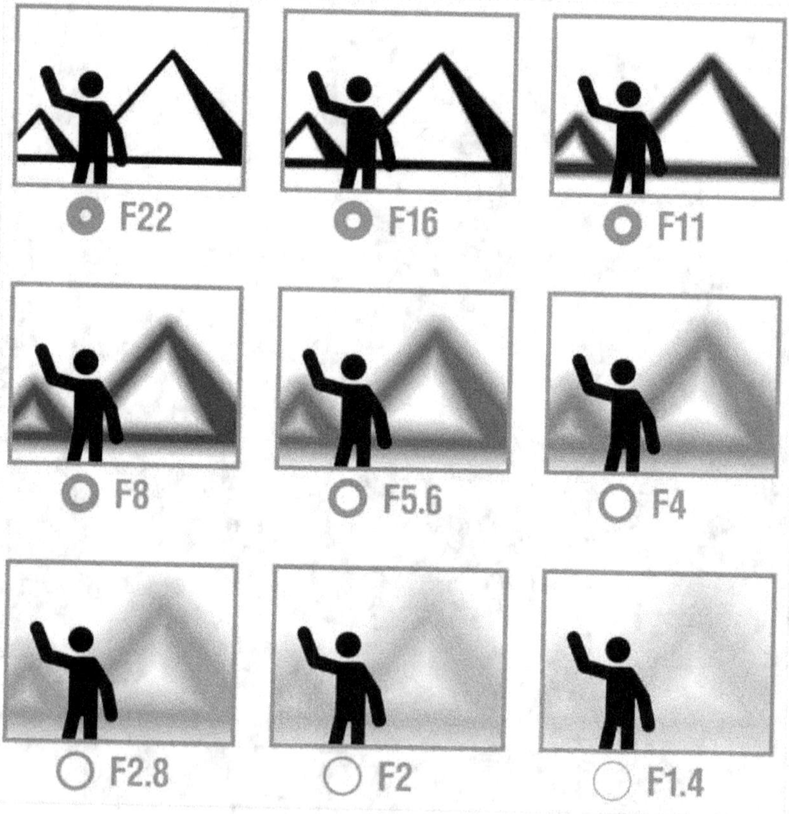

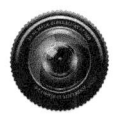

Technical settings

Reminder

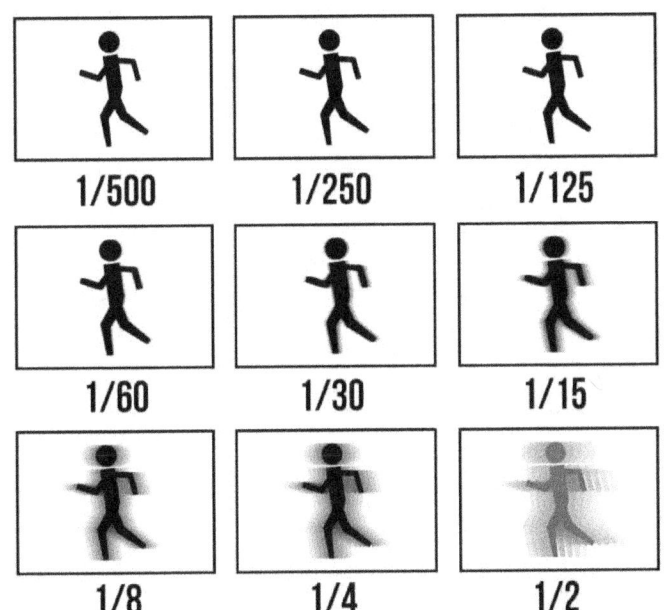

1/500	1/250	1/125
1/60	1/30	1/15
1/8	1/4	1/2

ISO

  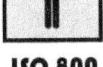 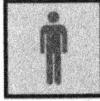 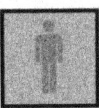

ISO 50	ISO 200	ISO 800	ISO 3200	ISO 12800

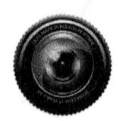

Technical settings

Cheat sheet

Indoor

Portrait Settings

1/60	f/4	ISO 800	Av(A)
minimum	your lowest	newer cameras	mode

Group Settings

1/80	f/7.1	ISO 800	Focus
minimum	for deep DOF	newer cameras	center-front person.

Sports Settings

1/800	f/2.8	ISO 1600	AI-Servo
minimum Av(A) mode	your lowest	or one-stop below highest	(AFC)

Outdoor

Sports Settings

1/1000	f/2.8	ISO 100	AI-Servo
minimum Av(A) mode	your lowest		(AFC)

Landscape Settings

Av(A)	f/16	ISO 100	Sunsets
mode Tripod	for deep DOF		(-) Exp. Comp.

Portrait Settings

1/60	f/2.8	ISO 200	Model
minimum Av(A) mode	to f/5.6		back to sun.

Group Settings

1/80	f/10	ISO 200	Focus
minimum Av(A) mode	for deep DOF	or one-stop below highest	center-front person.

Special

Flash Settings

1/200	f/8	ISO 100	Manual
maximum	good base	boost flash for more light	mode

Kids Settings

1/500	f/5.6	ISO 1600	AI-Servo
minimum Av(A) mode		good base	(AFC)

Night Settings

30"	f/14	ISO 400	Focus
or faster Manual mode	your lowest	adjust if needed.	manual

Close-up Settings

1/200	f/11	ISO 200	Tripod
Av(A) mode	or higher	or one-stop below highest	focus on what is closest.

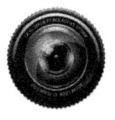

My settings

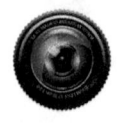

My equipment

_____
_____
_____
_____
_____
_____
_____
_____
_____
_____
_____
_____
_____
_____
_____
_____
_____
_____
_____

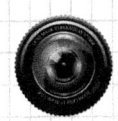

Creative Ideas

53 themes to remain inspired

1. In my hands
2. Texture
3. Travel
4. Coffee
5. Reflection
6. Faces
7. What I like
8. Blue
9. Light
10. Self portrait
11. Movement
12. Black & White
13. Mirror
14. Silhouette
15. Water
16. Between the lines
17. Small steps
18. Sweetness
19. View from above
20. What I read
21. My favorites
22. Landscape
23. Look
24. Animal
25. Fun
26. Closely
27. Memories
28. Sequins
29. My mood
30. Paper
31. Backlight
32. On the shelf
33. Colorful
34. Far away
35. Tiny
36. Childhood
37. The seasons
38. Numbers
39. Freedom
40. Close to you
41. Poetics
42. Upward
43. Curves
44. Dancing
45. Leaves
46. At night
47. Temptation
48. The day after
49. In my shoes
50. Fragile
51. Earth/soil
52. Balanced
53. Wait

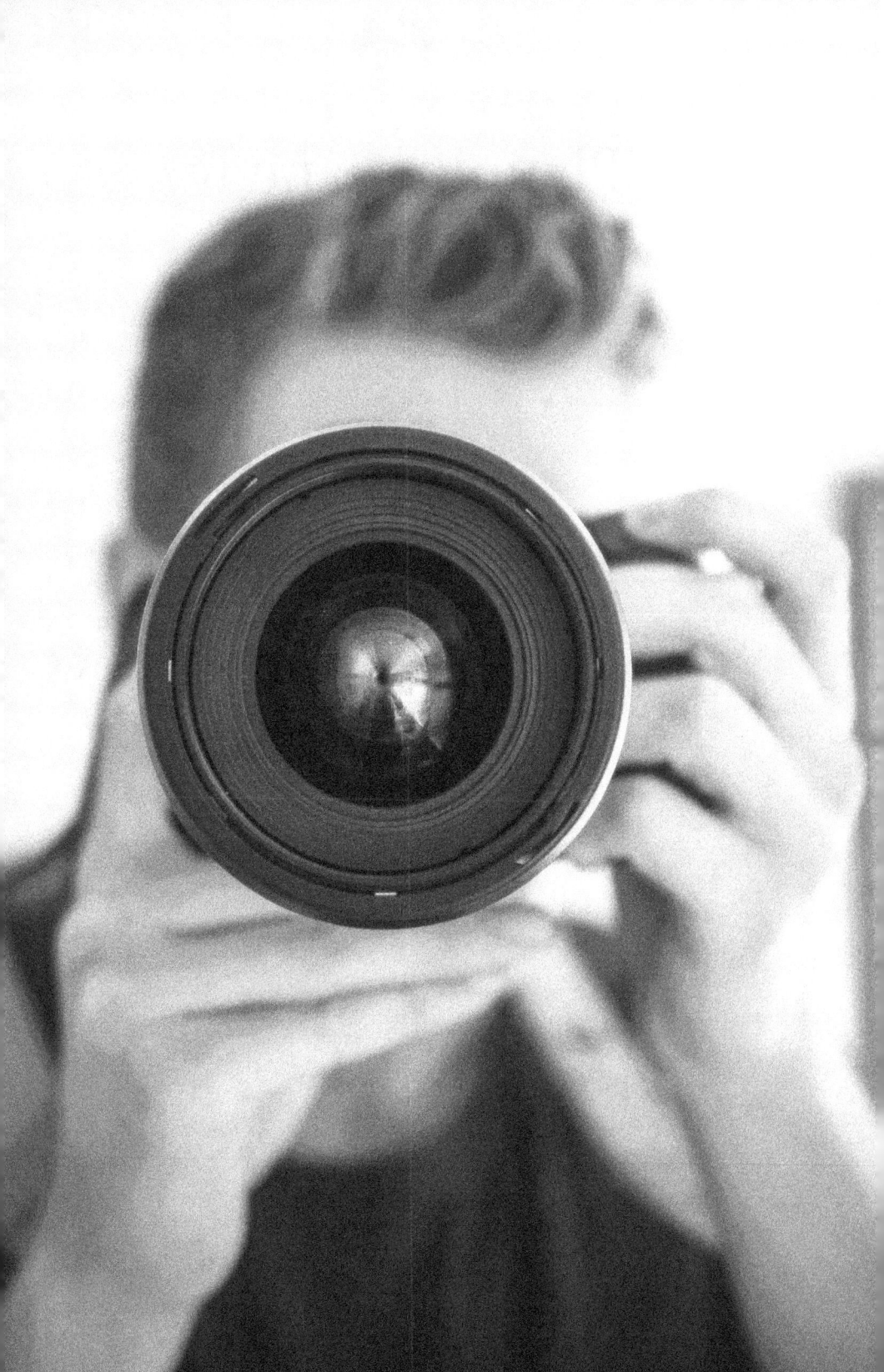

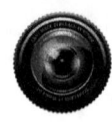

Planning January

M	T	W	T	F	S	S

GOAL OF THE MONTH

Notes

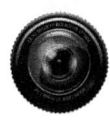

Planning February

M	T	W	T	F	S	S

GOAL OF THE MONTH

Notes

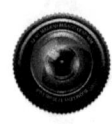

Planning March

M	T	W	T	F	S	S

GOAL OF THE MONTH

Notes

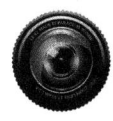

Planning April

M	T	W	T	F	S	S

GOAL OF THE MONTH

Notes

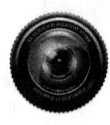

Planning May

M	T	W	T	F	S	S

GOAL OF THE MONTH

Notes

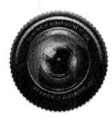

Planning June

M	T	W	T	F	S	S

GOAL OF THE MONTH

Notes

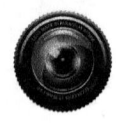

Planning July

M	T	W	T	F	S	S

GOAL OF THE MONTH

Notes

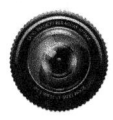

Planning August

M	T	W	T	F	S	S

GOAL OF THE MONTH

Notes

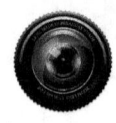

Planning September

M	T	W	T	F	S	S

GOAL OF THE MONTH

Notes

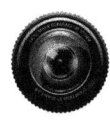

Planning October

M	T	W	T	F	S	S

GOAL OF THE MONTH

Notes

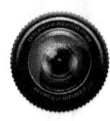

Planning November

M	T	W	T	F	S	S

GOAL OF THE MONTH

Notes

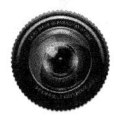

Planning December

M	T	W	T	F	S	S

GOAL OF THE MONTH

Notes

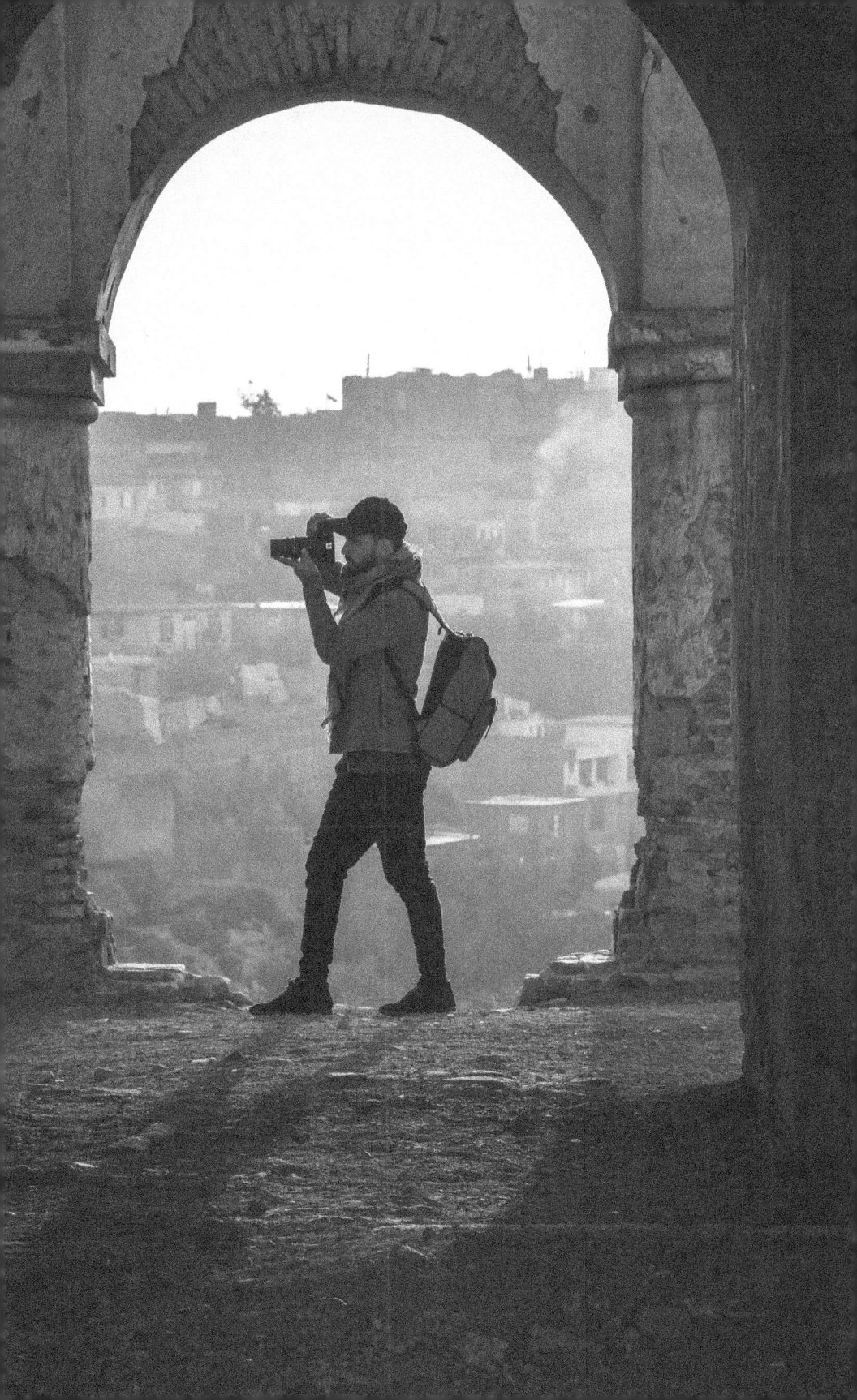

Mind Map

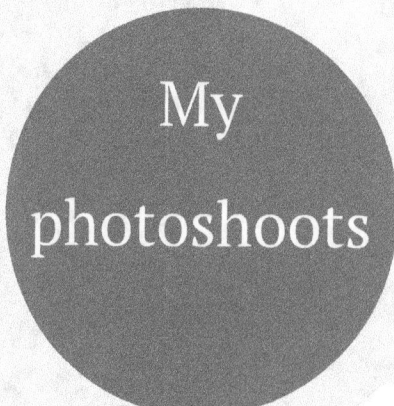

My photoshoots

DEFINE THE GOAL

. Rendering (Theme, Ambiance, Colors)
. Timing
. Publishing (Social networks, Website, media,...)
. Exhibition
. ...

CREATE A MOOD BOARD

. Inspiration (Pinterest ...)
. Create the moodboard
. List all scenes & define shooting blueprint

CHOSE THE TEAM

. Model.s
. Stylist
. Make Up Artist
. Hairdresser
. Assistant
. ...

DEFINE LOCATION/ DATE

. Select location (Studio indoor/ Outdoor)
. Address / authorization
. Date / Time (Golden Hour)

CHOSE STYLING

. Accessories
. Clothes
. Jewelry
. Shoes
. ...

DEFINE DECORATION

. Flowers
. Furniture
. Blanket
. Curtain
. ...

PREPARE THE SHOOTING

. Technical settings

SELECT EQUIPMENT

. Backgrounds
. DSLR / Lenses
. Flash
. UV Filter
. ...

PHOTO EDITING

Retouching/ Presets :
. Lightroom
. Photoshop

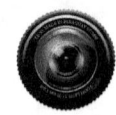

Summary
of my photo shooting
sheets

N°	SHOOTING NAME & DESCRIPTION	✓
1		☐
2		☐
3		☐
4		☐
5		☐
6		☐
7		☐
8		☐
9		☐
10		☐
11		☐
12		☐
13		☐
14		☐
15		☐

NOTES

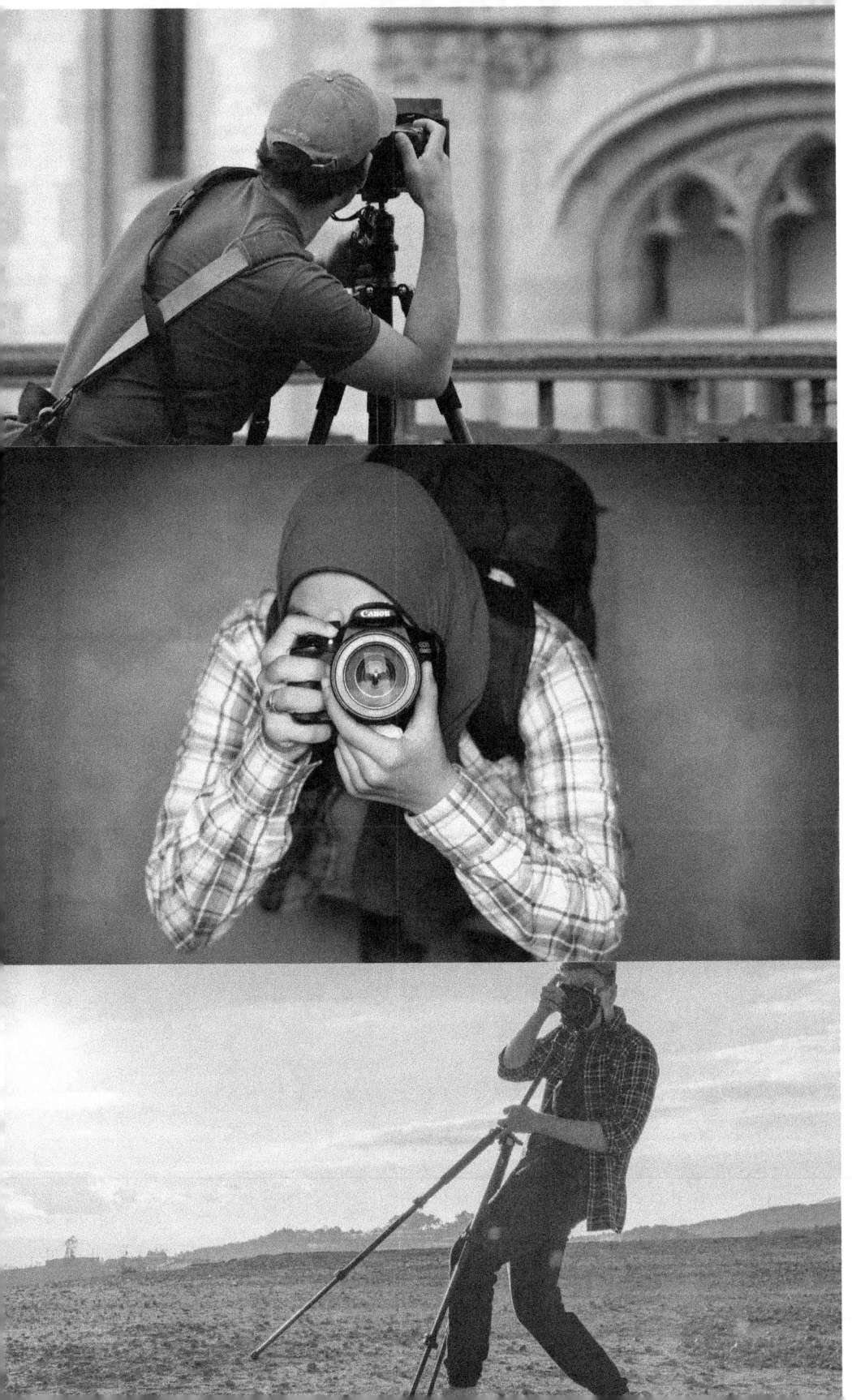

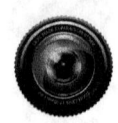

Shooting Sheet n°1

SHOOTING NAME

DESCRIPTION

PHOTO SHOOTING GOAL

LOCATION   TIME

ADDRESS

AUTHORIZATION(S) REQUIRED ? (Y/N)

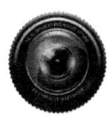

Shooting Sheet n°1

MY TEAM
MODEL(S), STYLIST, MAKE UP ARTIST, HAIRDRESSER, ...

FASHION DESIGN
CLOTHES, JEWELRY, SHOES...

DECORATION
FLOWERS, FURNITURE, ACCESSORIES, ...

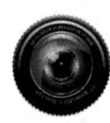

Shooting Sheet n°1

MY INSPIRATIONS

MY MOODBOARD

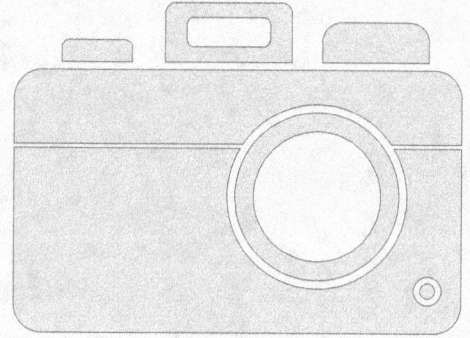

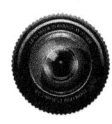

Shooting Sheet n°1

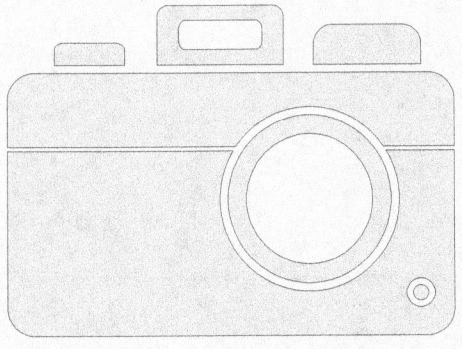

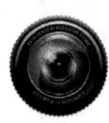

Shooting Sheet n°1

PHOTO SHOOTING

TECHNICAL SETTINGS

EQUIPMENT

PHOTO EDITING

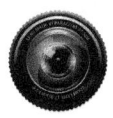

Shooting Sheet n°1

LIST OF SCENES & PLANS

_____

_____

_____

_____

_____

_____

_____

_____

_____

_____

_____

_____

_____

_____

_____

_____

_____

_____

_____

_____

_____

_____

_____

_____

_____

_____

_____

_____

_____

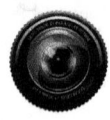

Shooting Sheet n°1

PUBLICATIONS

Notes

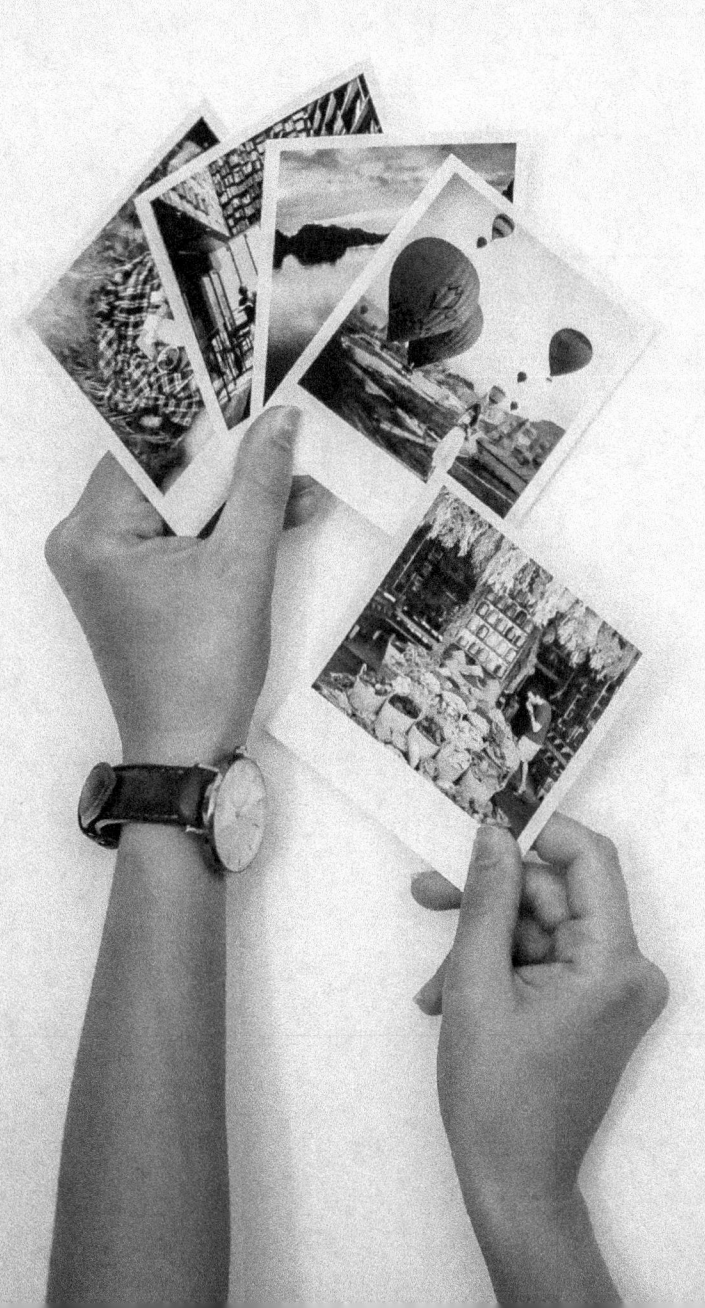

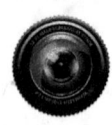

Shooting Sheet n°2

SHOOTING NAME

DESCRIPTION

PHOTO SHOOTING GOAL

LOCATION   TIME

ADDRESS

AUTHORIZATION(S) REQUIRED ? (Y/N)

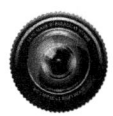

Shooting Sheet n°2

MY TEAM
MODEL(S), STYLIST, MAKE UP ARTIST, HAIRDRESSER, ...

FASHION DESIGN
CLOTHES, JEWELRY, SHOES...

DECORATION
FLOWERS, FURNITURE, ACCESSORIES, ...

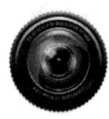

Shooting Sheet n°2

MY INSPIRATIONS

MY MOODBOARD

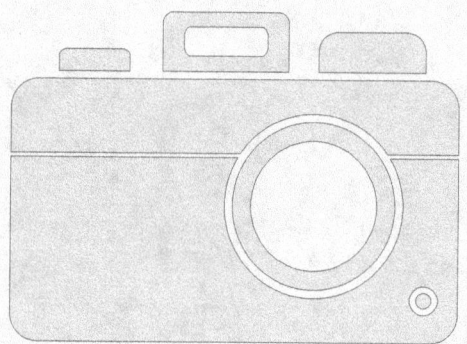

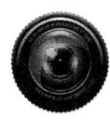

Shooting Sheet n°2

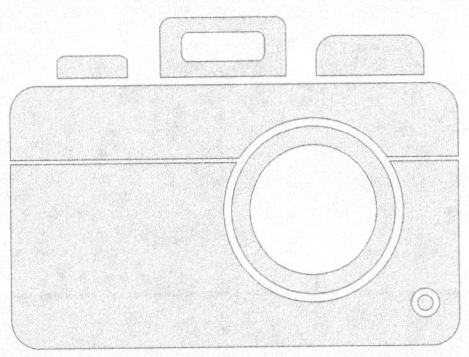

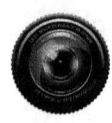

Shooting Sheet n°2

PHOTO SHOOTING

TECHNICAL SETTINGS

EQUIPMENT

PHOTO EDITING

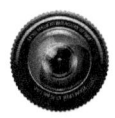

Shooting Sheet n°2

LIST OF SCENES & PLANS

_____
_____
_____
_____
_____
_____
_____
_____
_____
_____
_____
_____
_____
_____
_____
_____
_____
_____
_____
_____
_____
_____
_____
_____

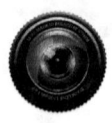

Shooting Sheet n°2

Notes

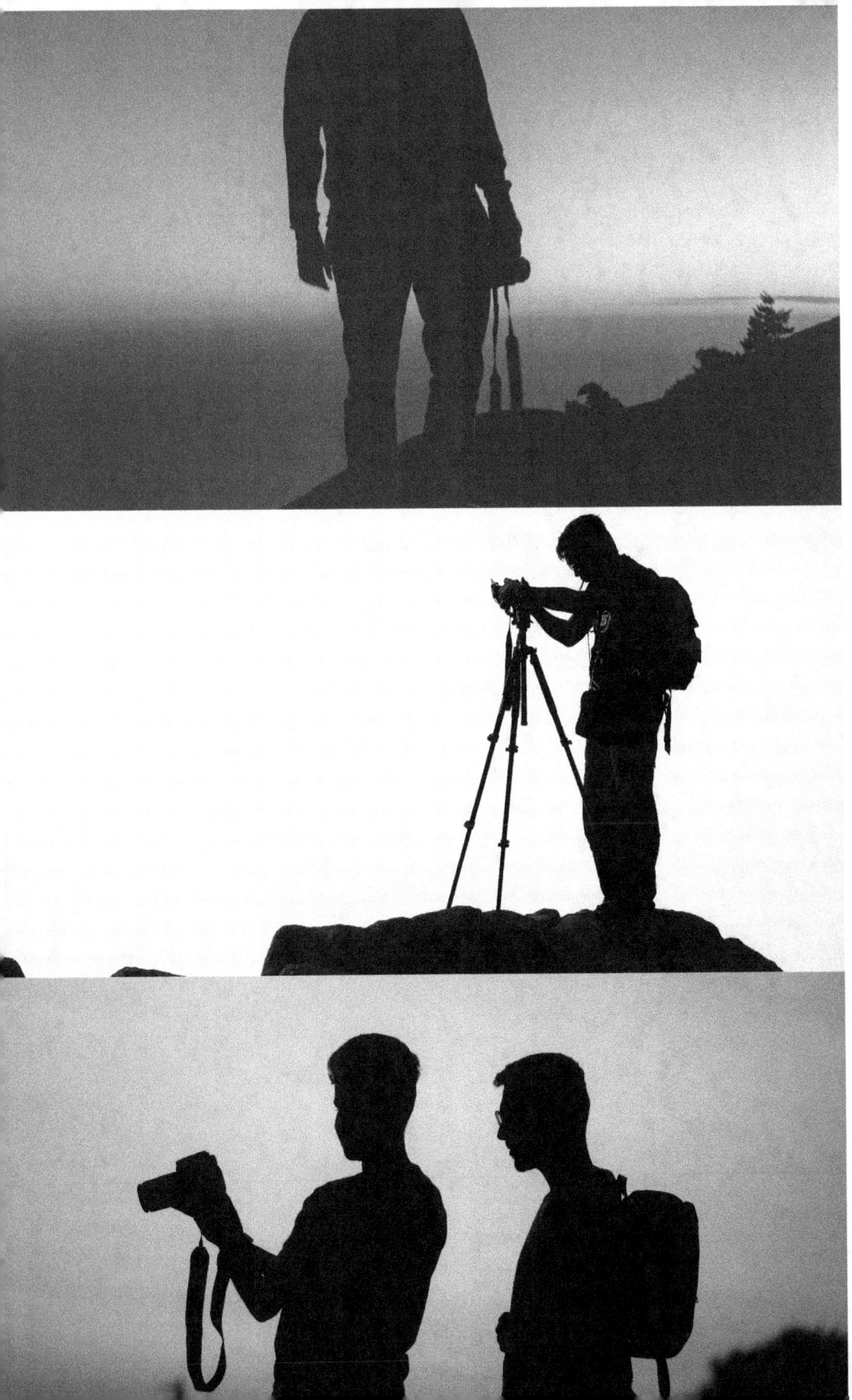

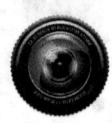

Shooting Sheet n°3

SHOOTING NAME

DESCRIPTION

PHOTO SHOOTING GOAL

LOCATION   TIME

ADDRESS

AUTHORIZATION(S) REQUIRED ? (Y/N)

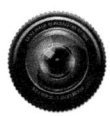

Shooting Sheet n°3

MY TEAM
MODEL(S), STYLIST, MAKE UP ARTIST, HAIRDRESSER, ...

FASHION DESIGN
CLOTHES, JEWELRY, SHOES...

DECORATION
FLOWERS, FURNITURE, ACCESSORIES, ...

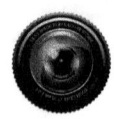

Shooting Sheet n°3

MY INSPIRATIONS

MY MOODBOARD

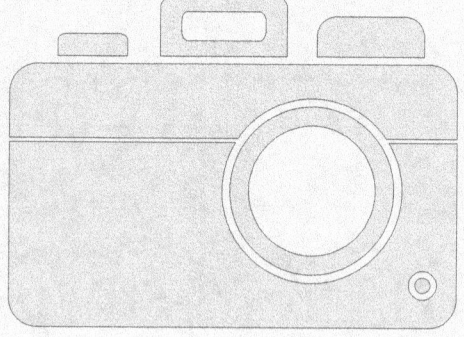

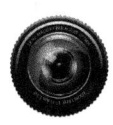

Shooting Sheet n°3

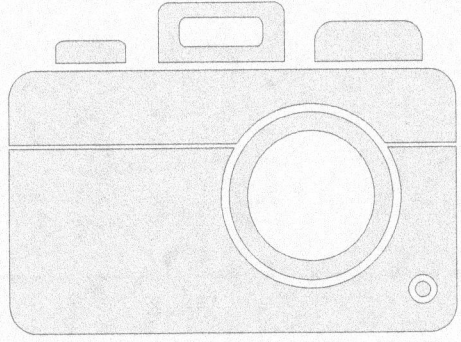

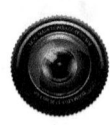

Shooting Sheet n°3

PHOTO SHOOTING

TECHNICAL SETTINGS

EQUIPMENT

PHOTO EDITING

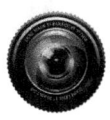

Shooting Sheet n°3

LIST OF SCENES & PLANS

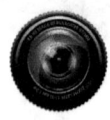

Shooting Sheet n°3

PUBLICATIONS

Notes

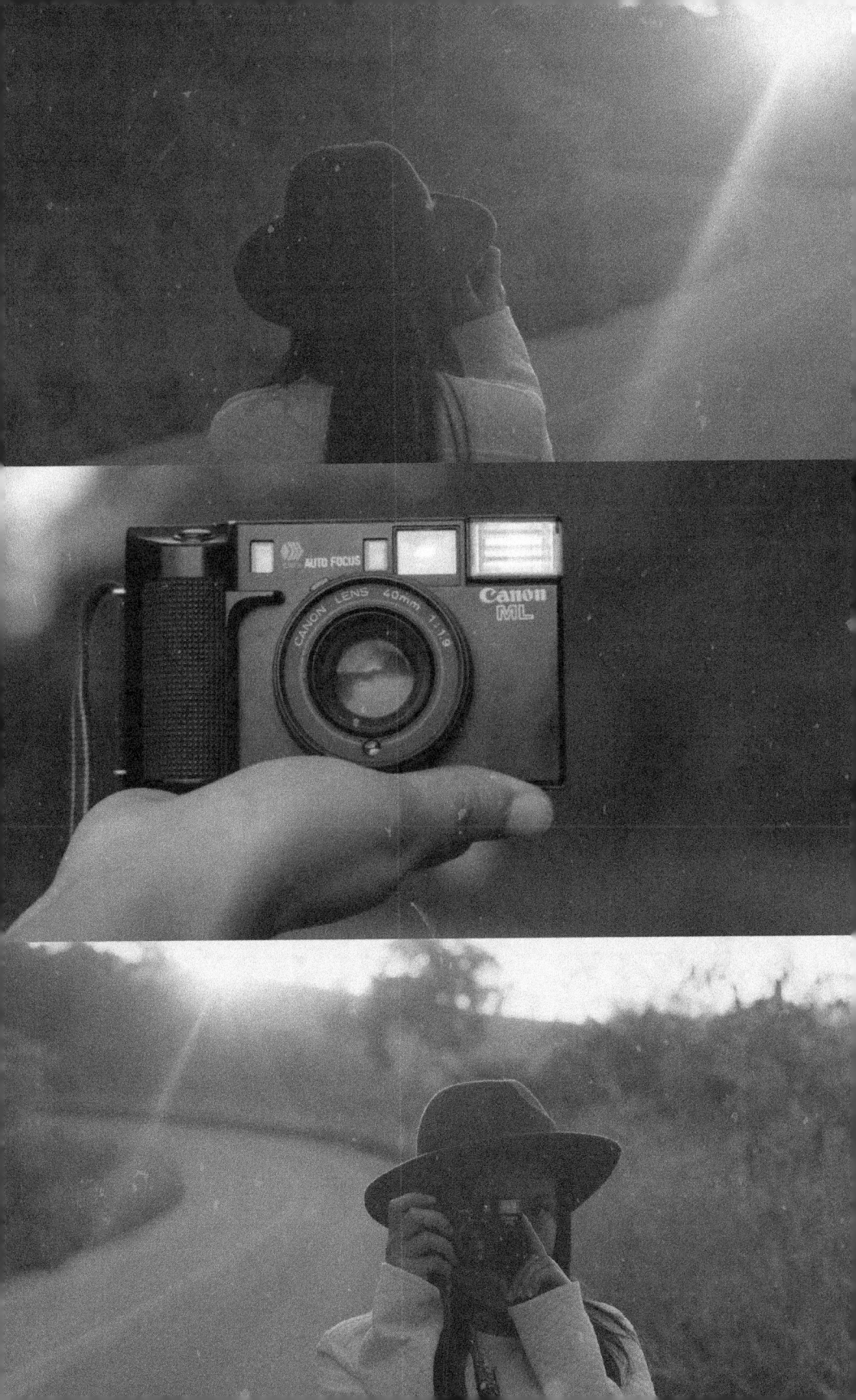

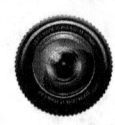

Shooting Sheet n°4

SHOOTING NAME

DESCRIPTION

PHOTO SHOOTING GOAL

LOCATION

TIME

ADDRESS

AUTHORIZATION(S) REQUIRED ? (Y/N)

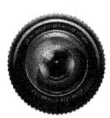

Shooting Sheet n°4

MY TEAM
MODEL(S), STYLIST, MAKE UP ARTIST, HAIRDRESSER, ...

FASHION DESIGN
CLOTHES, JEWELRY, SHOES...

DECORATION
FLOWERS, FURNITURE, ACCESSORIES, ...

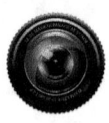

Shooting Sheet n°4

MY INSPIRATIONS

MY MOODBOARD

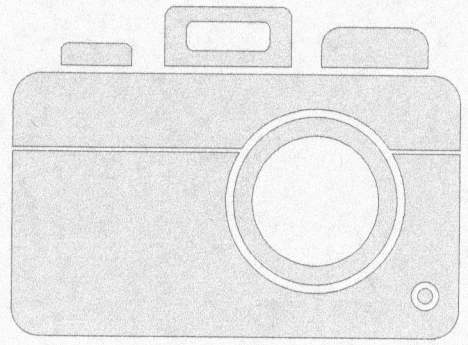

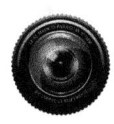

Shooting Sheet n°4

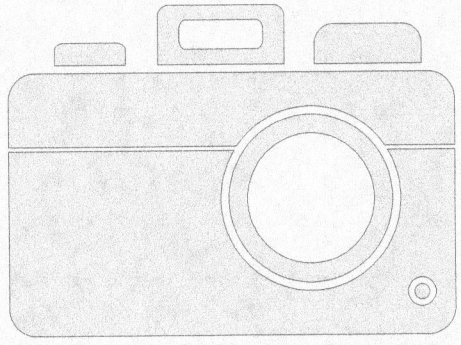

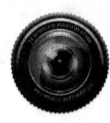

Shooting Sheet n°4

PHOTO SHOOTING

TECHNICAL SETTINGS

EQUIPMENT

PHOTO EDITING

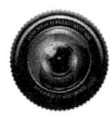

Shooting Sheet n°4

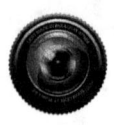

Shooting Sheet n°4

Notes

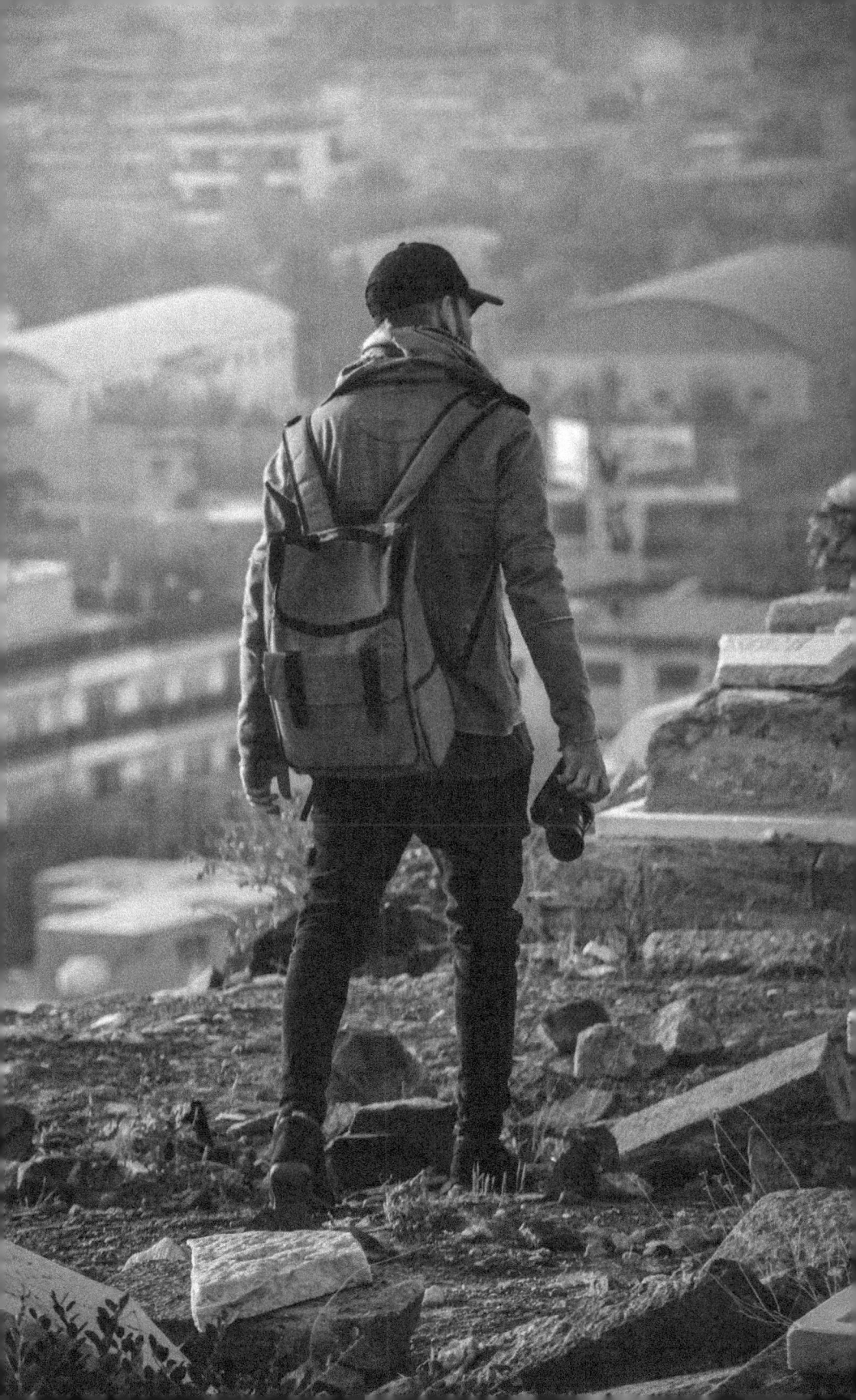

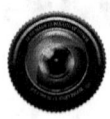

Shooting Sheet n°5

SHOOTING NAME
_____

DESCRIPTION

PHOTO SHOOTING GOAL
_____

LOCATION   TIME
_____

ADDRESS

AUTHORIZATION(S) REQUIRED ? (Y/N)

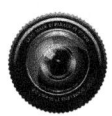

Shooting Sheet n°5

MY TEAM
MODEL(S), STYLIST, MAKE UP ARTIST, HAIRDRESSER, ...

FASHION DESIGN
CLOTHES, JEWELRY, SHOES...

DECORATION
FLOWERS, FURNITURE, ACCESSORIES, ...

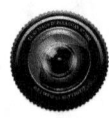

Shooting Sheet n°5

MY INSPIRATIONS

MY MOODBOARD

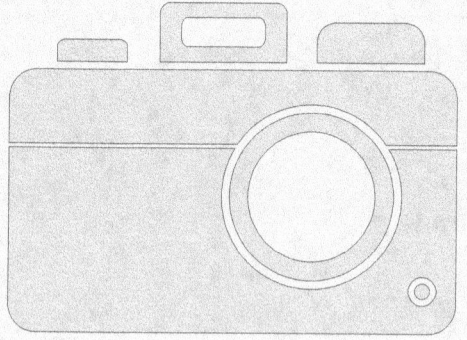

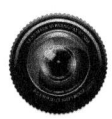

Shooting Sheet n°5

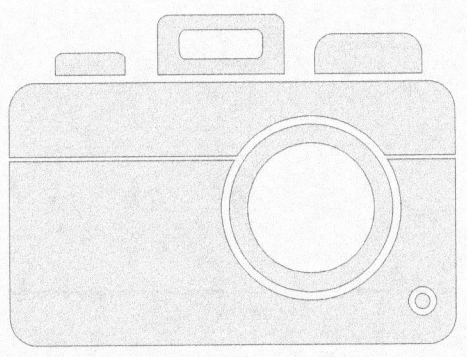

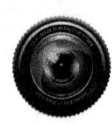

Shooting Sheet n°5

PHOTO SHOOTING

TECHNICAL SETTINGS

EQUIPMENT

PHOTO EDITING

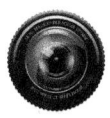

Shooting Sheet n°5

LIST OF SCENES & PLANS

_____
_____
_____
_____
_____
_____
_____
_____
_____
_____
_____
_____
_____
_____
_____
_____
_____
_____
_____
_____
_____
_____
_____

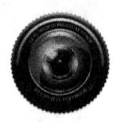

Shooting Sheet n°5

PUBLICATIONS

Notes

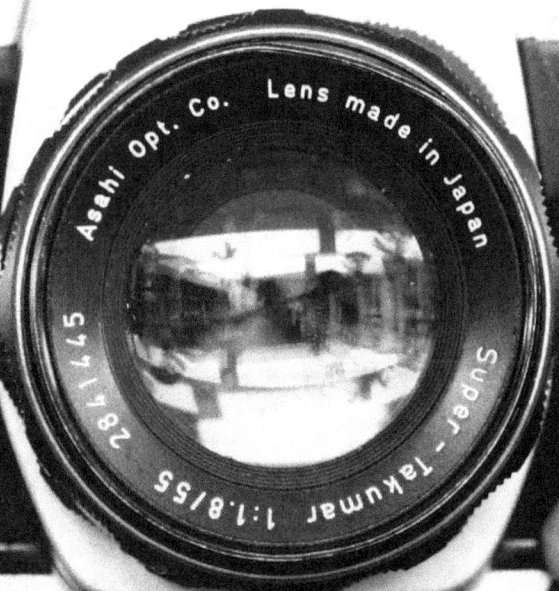

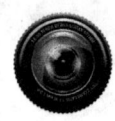

Shooting Sheet n°6

SHOOTING NAME

DESCRIPTION

PHOTO SHOOTING GOAL

LOCATION   TIME

ADDRESS

AUTHORIZATION(S) REQUIRED ? (Y/N)

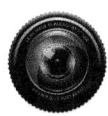

Shooting Sheet n°6

MY TEAM

MODEL(S), STYLIST, MAKE UP ARTIST, HAIRDRESSER, ...

FASHION DESIGN

CLOTHES, JEWELRY, SHOES...

DECORATION

FLOWERS, FURNITURE, ACCESSORIES, ...

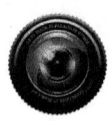

Shooting Sheet n°6

MY INSPIRATIONS

MY MOODBOARD

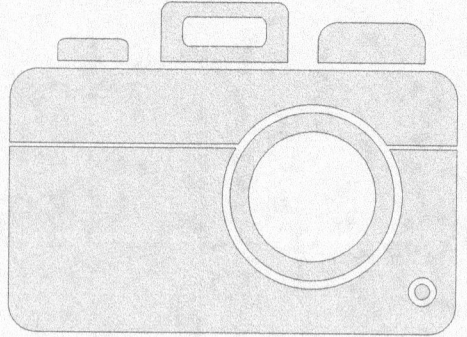

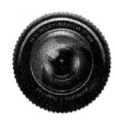

Shooting Sheet n°6

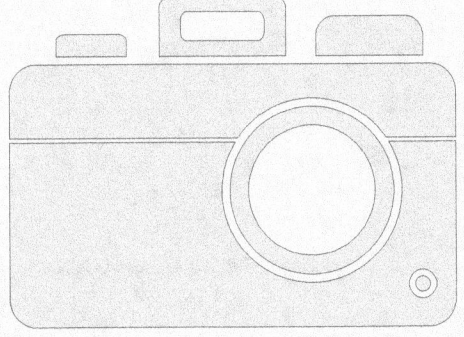

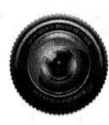

Shooting Sheet n°6

PHOTO SHOOTING

TECHNICAL SETTINGS

EQUIPMENT

PHOTO EDITING

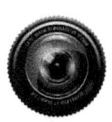

Shooting Sheet n°6

LIST OF SCENES & PLANS

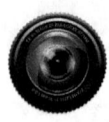

Shooting Sheet n°6

PUBLICATIONS

Notes

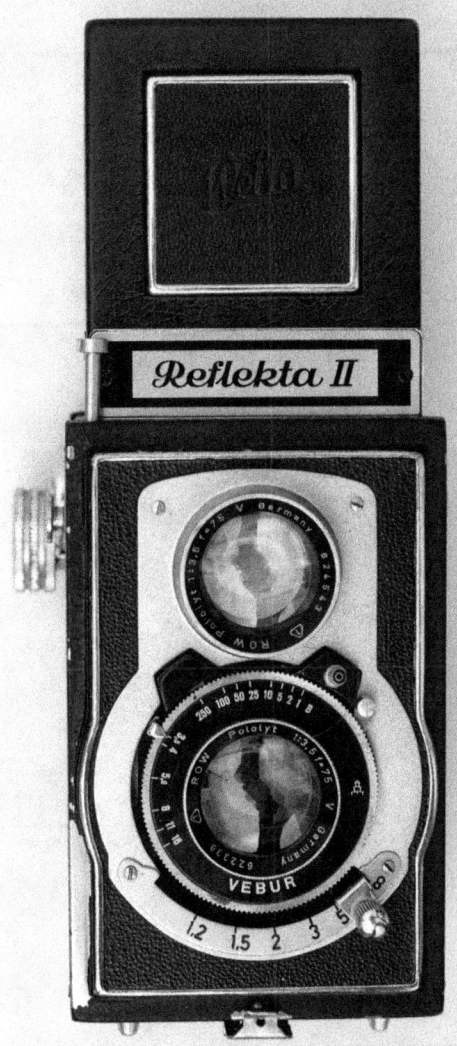

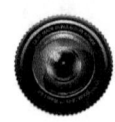

Shooting Sheet n°7

SHOOTING NAME

DESCRIPTION

PHOTO SHOOTING GOAL

LOCATION   TIME

ADDRESS

AUTHORIZATION(S) REQUIRED ? (Y/N)

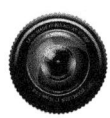

Shooting Sheet n°7

MY TEAM
MODEL(S), STYLIST, MAKE UP ARTIST, HAIRDRESSER, ...

FASHION DESIGN
CLOTHES, JEWELRY, SHOES...

DECORATION
FLOWERS, FURNITURE, ACCESSORIES, ...

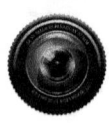

Shooting Sheet n°7

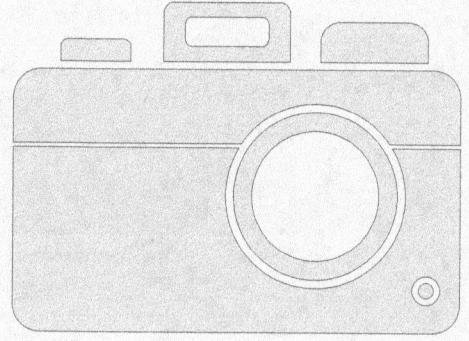

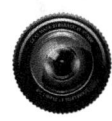

Shooting Sheet n°7

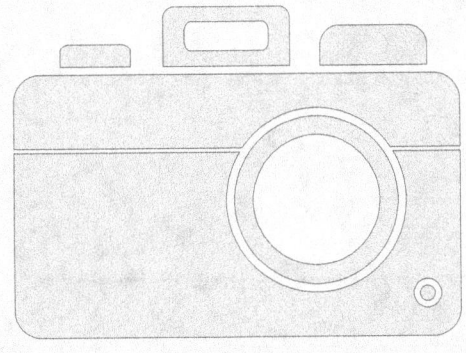

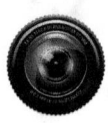

Shooting Sheet n°7

PHOTO SHOOTING

TECHNICAL SETTINGS

EQUIPMENT

PHOTO EDITING

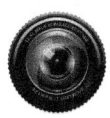

Shooting Sheet n°7

LIST OF SCENES & PLANS

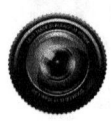

Shooting Sheet n°7

PUBLICATIONS

Notes

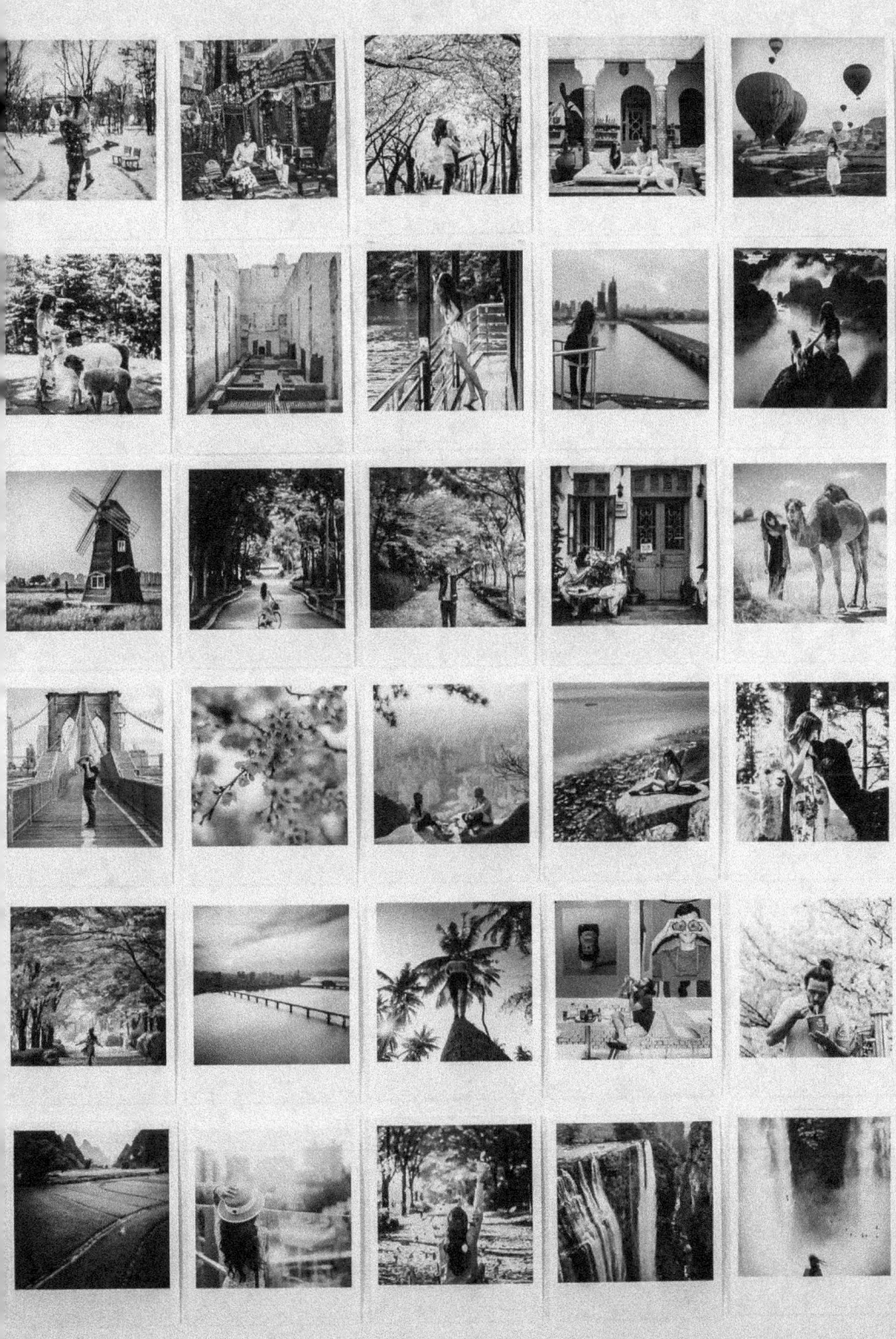

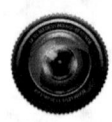

Shooting Sheet n°8

SHOOTING NAME

DESCRIPTION

PHOTO SHOOTING GOAL

LOCATION

TIME

ADDRESS

AUTHORIZATION(S) REQUIRED ? (Y/N)

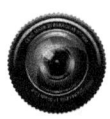

Shooting Sheet n°8

MY TEAM
MODEL(S), STYLIST, MAKE UP ARTIST, HAIRDRESSER, ...

FASHION DESIGN
CLOTHES, JEWELRY, SHOES...

DECORATION
FLOWERS, FURNITURE, ACCESSORIES, ...

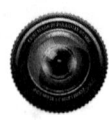

Shooting Sheet n°8

MY INSPIRATIONS

MY MOODBOARD

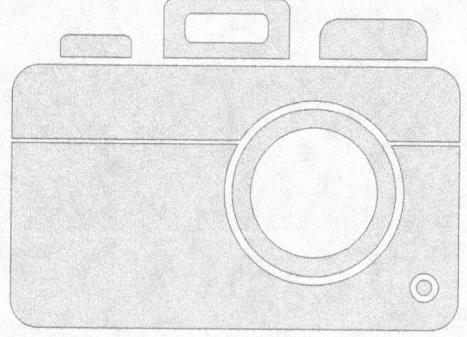

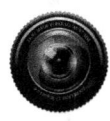

Shooting Sheet n°8

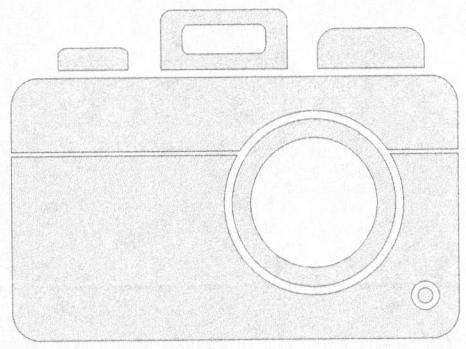

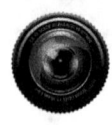

Shooting Sheet n°8

PHOTO SHOOTING

TECHNICAL SETTINGS

EQUIPMENT

PHOTO EDITING

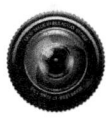

Shooting Sheet n°8

_____
_____
_____
_____
_____
_____
_____
_____
_____
_____
_____
_____
_____
_____
_____
_____
_____
_____
_____
_____
_____
_____

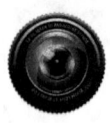

Shooting Sheet n°8

PUBLICATIONS

Notes

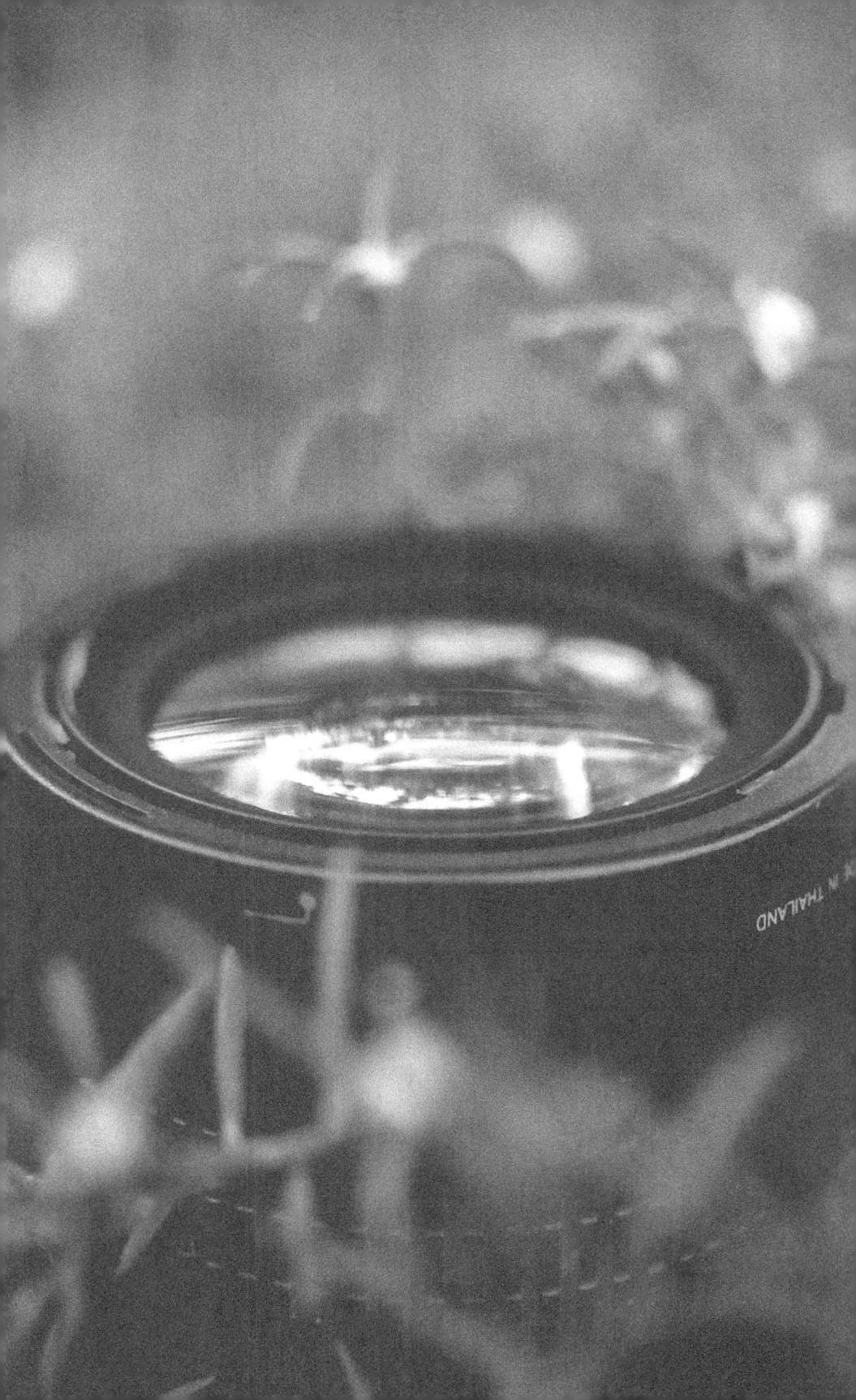

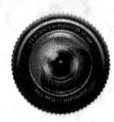

Shooting Sheet n°9

SHOOTING NAME

DESCRIPTION

PHOTO SHOOTING GOAL

LOCATION

TIME

ADDRESS

AUTHORIZATION(S) REQUIRED ? (Y/N)

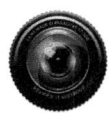

Shooting Sheet n°9

MY TEAM
MODEL(S), STYLIST, MAKE UP ARTIST, HAIRDRESSER, ...

FASHION DESIGN
CLOTHES, JEWELRY, SHOES...

DECORATION
FLOWERS, FURNITURE, ACCESSORIES, ...

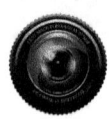

Shooting Sheet n°9

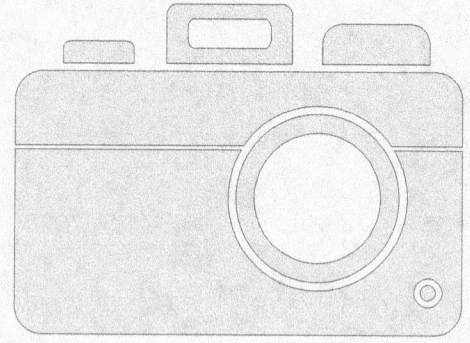

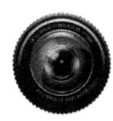

Shooting Sheet n°9

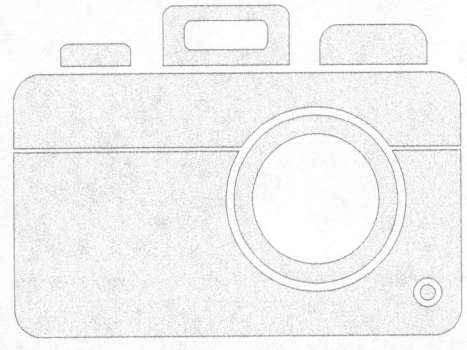

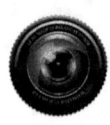

Shooting Sheet n°9

PHOTO SHOOTING

TECHNICAL SETTINGS

EQUIPMENT

PHOTO EDITING

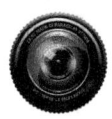

Shooting Sheet n°9

LIST OF SCENES & PLANS

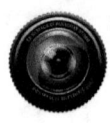

Shooting Sheet n°9

Notes

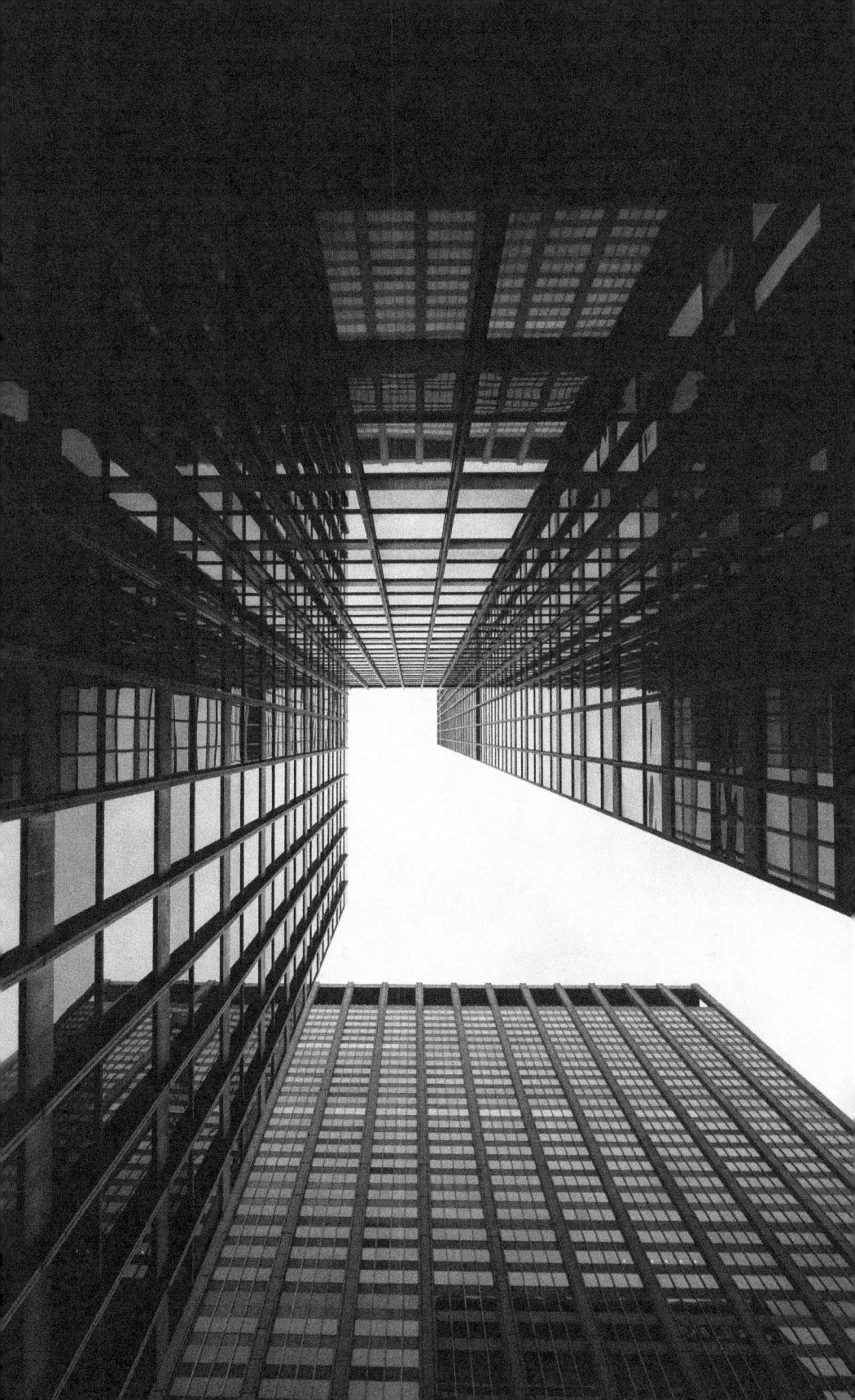

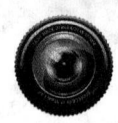

Shooting Sheet n°10

SHOOTING NAME

DESCRIPTION

PHOTO SHOOTING GOAL

LOCATION

TIME

ADDRESS

AUTHORIZATION(S) REQUIRED ? (Y/N)

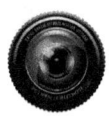

Shooting Sheet n°10

MY TEAM
MODEL(S), STYLIST, MAKE UP ARTIST, HAIRDRESSER, ...

FASHION DESIGN
CLOTHES, JEWELRY, SHOES...

DECORATION
FLOWERS, FURNITURE, ACCESSORIES, ...

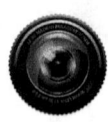

Shooting Sheet n°10

MY INSPIRATIONS

MY MOODBOARD

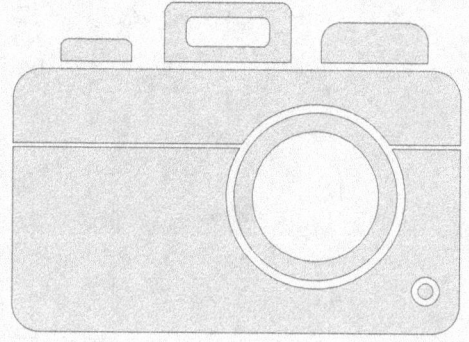

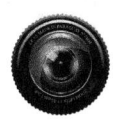

Shooting Sheet n°10

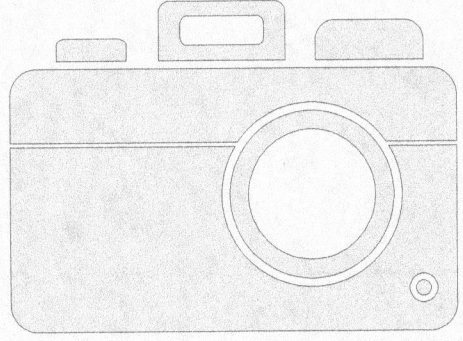

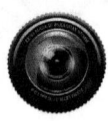

Shooting Sheet n°10

PHOTO SHOOTING

TECHNICAL SETTINGS

EQUIPMENT

PHOTO EDITING

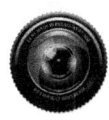

Shooting Sheet n°10

LIST OF SCENES & PLANS

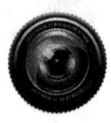

Shooting Sheet n°10

Notes

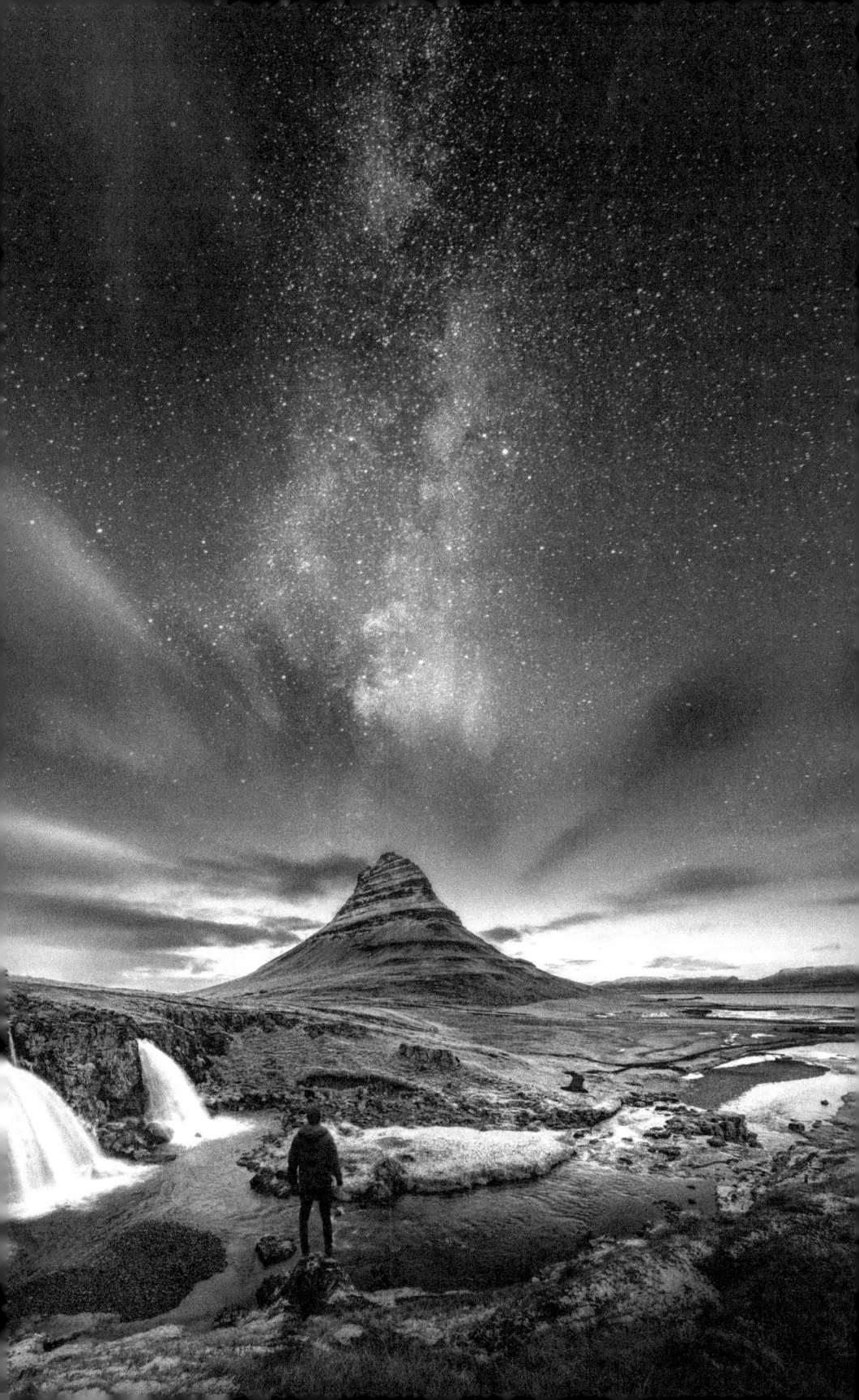

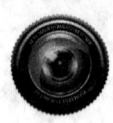

Shooting Sheet n°11

SHOOTING NAME

DESCRIPTION

PHOTO SHOOTING GOAL

LOCATION

TIME

ADDRESS

AUTHORIZATION(S) REQUIRED ? (Y/N)

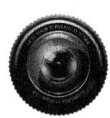

Shooting Sheet n°11

MY TEAM
MODEL(S), STYLIST, MAKE UP ARTIST, HAIRDRESSER, ...

FASHION DESIGN
CLOTHES, JEWELRY, SHOES...

DECORATION
FLOWERS, FURNITURE, ACCESSORIES, ...

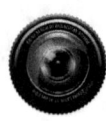

Shooting Sheet n°11

MY INSPIRATIONS

MY MOODBOARD

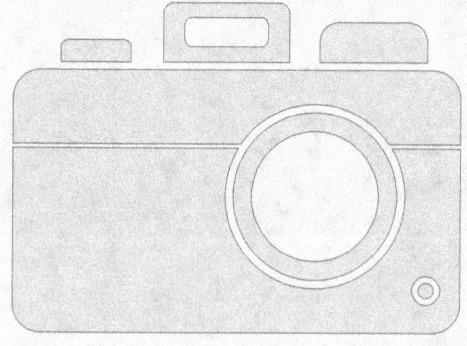

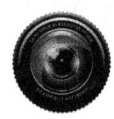

Shooting Sheet n°11

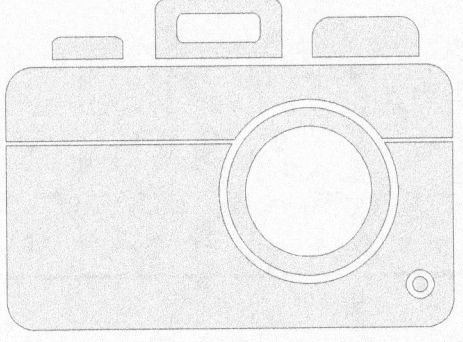

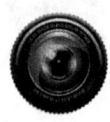

Shooting Sheet n°11

PHOTO SHOOTING

TECHNICAL SETTINGS

EQUIPMENT

PHOTO EDITING

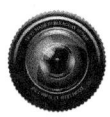

Shooting Sheet n°11

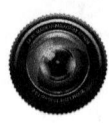

Shooting Sheet n°11

PUBLICATIONS

Notes

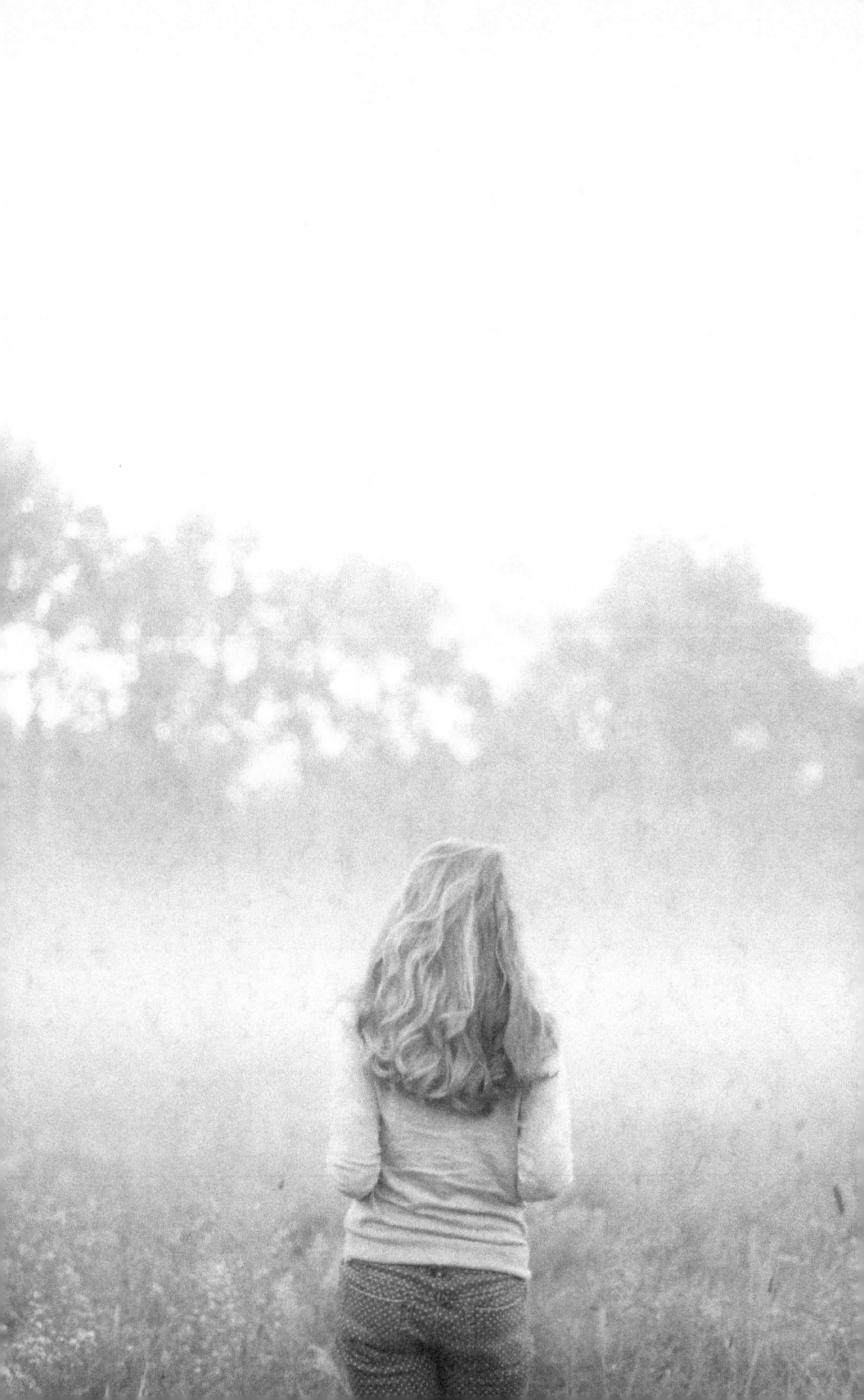

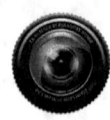

Shooting Sheet n°12

SHOOTING NAME

DESCRIPTION

PHOTO SHOOTING GOAL

LOCATION

TIME

ADDRESS

AUTHORIZATION(S) REQUIRED ? (Y/N)

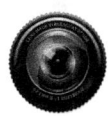

Shooting Sheet n°12

MY TEAM
MODEL(S), STYLIST, MAKE UP ARTIST, HAIRDRESSER, ...

FASHION DESIGN
CLOTHES, JEWELRY, SHOES...

DECORATION
FLOWERS, FURNITURE, ACCESSORIES, ...

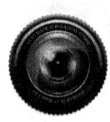

Shooting Sheet n°12

MY INSPIRATIONS

MY MOODBOARD

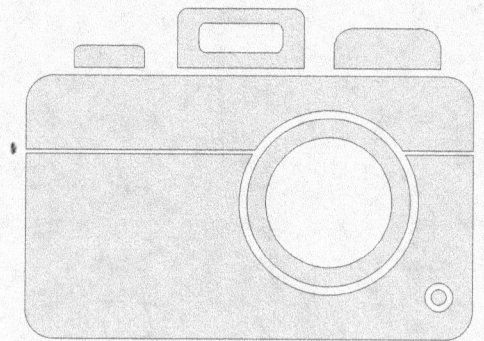

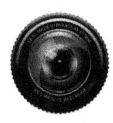

Shooting Sheet n°12

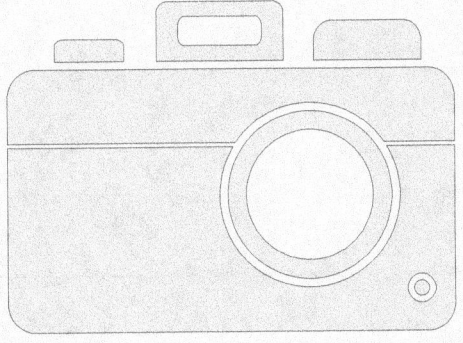

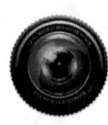

Shooting Sheet n°12

PHOTO SHOOTING

TECHNICAL SETTINGS

EQUIPMENT

PHOTO EDITING

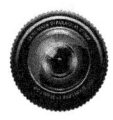

Shooting Sheet n°12

LIST OF SCENES & PLANS

_____

_____

_____

_____

_____

_____

_____

_____

_____

_____

_____

_____

_____

_____

_____

_____

_____

_____

_____

_____

_____

_____

_____

_____

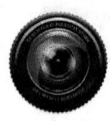

Shooting Sheet n°12

Notes

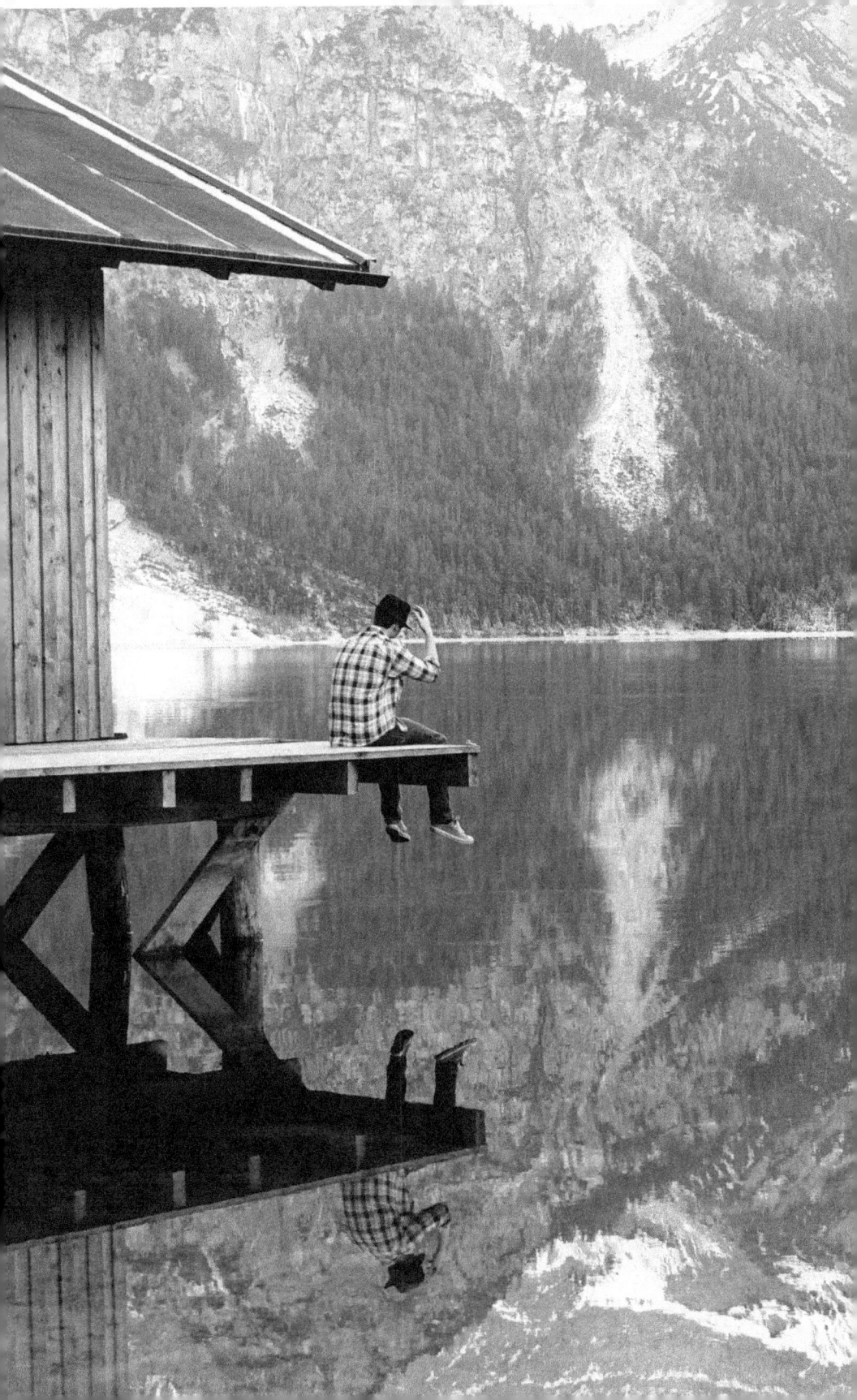

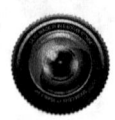

Shooting Sheet n°13

SHOOTING NAME

DESCRIPTION

PHOTO SHOOTING GOAL

LOCATION

TIME

ADDRESS

AUTHORIZATION(S) REQUIRED ? (Y/N)

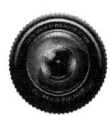

Shooting Sheet n°13

MY TEAM
MODEL(S), STYLIST, MAKE UP ARTIST, HAIRDRESSER, ...

FASHION DESIGN
CLOTHES, JEWELRY, SHOES...

DECORATION
FLOWERS, FURNITURE, ACCESSORIES, ...

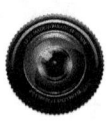

Shooting Sheet n°13

MY INSPIRATIONS

MY MOODBOARD

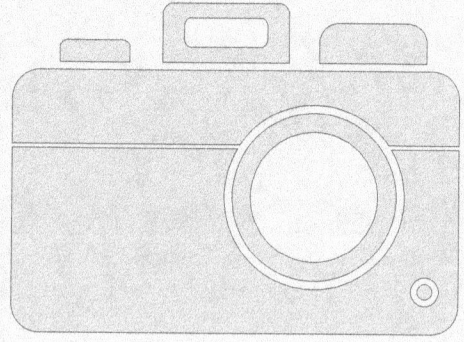

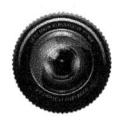

Shooting Sheet n°13

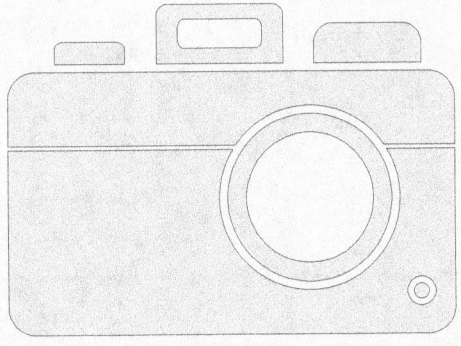

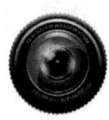

Shooting Sheet n°13

PHOTO SHOOTING

TECHNICAL SETTINGS

EQUIPMENT

PHOTO EDITING

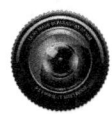

Shooting Sheet n°13

LIST OF SCENES & PLANS

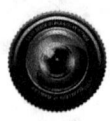

Shooting Sheet n°13

Notes

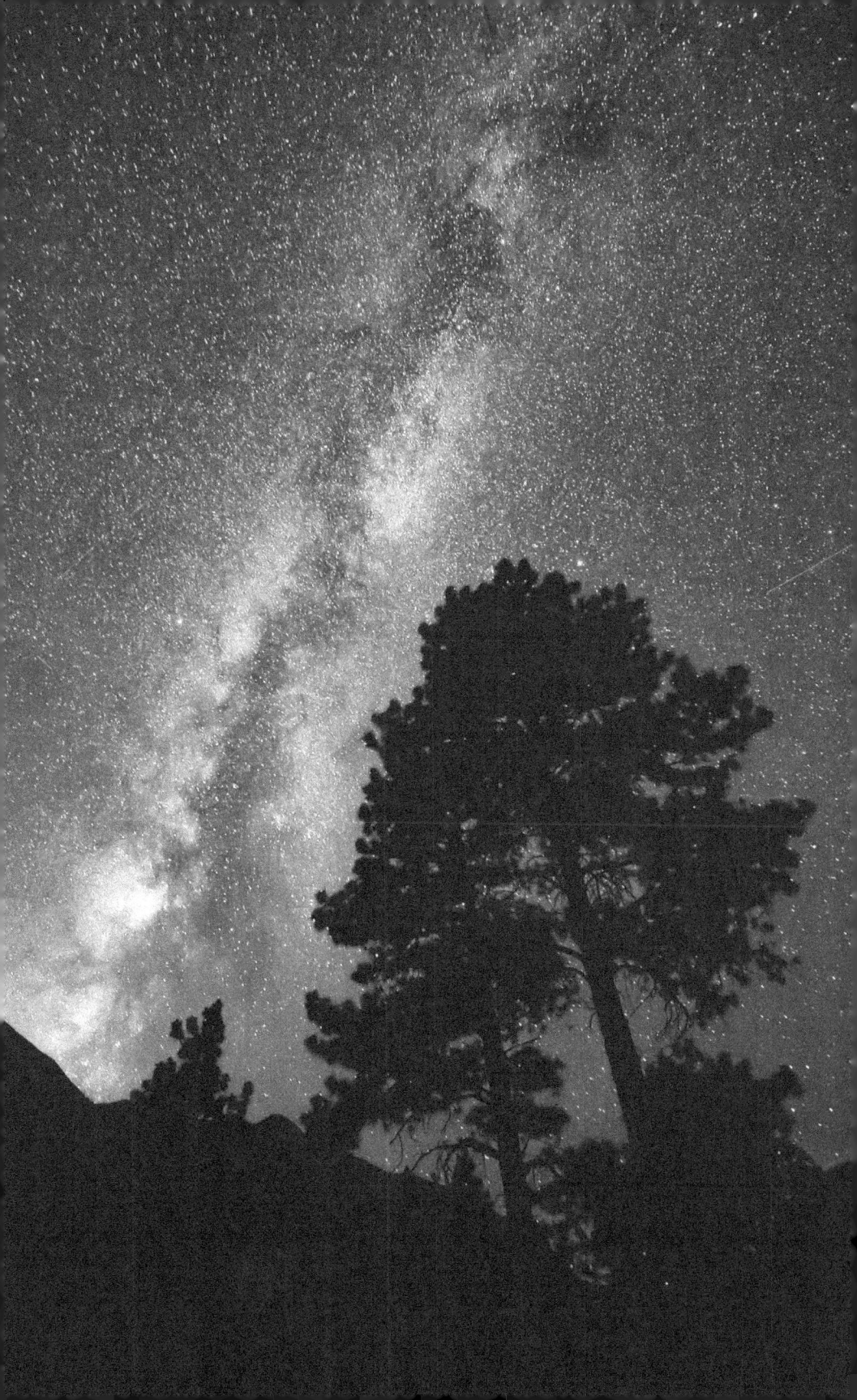

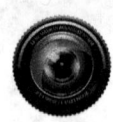

Shooting Sheet n°14

SHOOTING NAME

DESCRIPTION

PHOTO SHOOTING GOAL

LOCATION

TIME

ADDRESS

AUTHORIZATION(S) REQUIRED ? (Y/N)

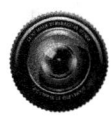

Shooting Sheet n°14

MY TEAM
MODEL(S), STYLIST, MAKE UP ARTIST, HAIRDRESSER, ...

FASHION DESIGN
CLOTHES, JEWELRY, SHOES...

DECORATION
FLOWERS, FURNITURE, ACCESSORIES, ...

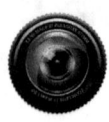

Shooting Sheet n°14

MY INSPIRATIONS

MY MOODBOARD

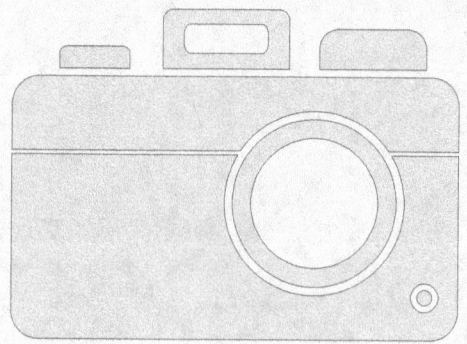

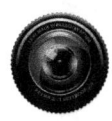

Shooting Sheet n°14

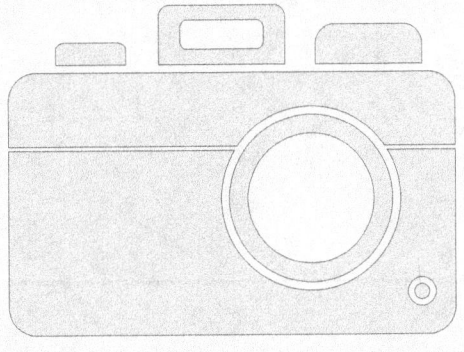

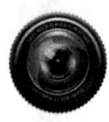

Shooting Sheet n°14

PHOTO SHOOTING

TECHNICAL SETTINGS

EQUIPMENT

PHOTO EDITING

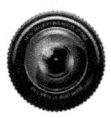

Shooting Sheet n°14

LIST OF SCENES & PLANS

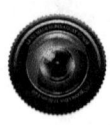

Shooting Sheet n°14

PUBLICATIONS

Notes

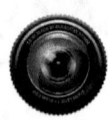

Shooting Sheet n°15

SHOOTING NAME

DESCRIPTION

PHOTO SHOOTING GOAL

LOCATION

TIME

ADDRESS

AUTHORIZATION(S) REQUIRED ? (Y/N)

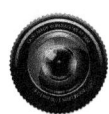

Shooting Sheet n°15

MY TEAM
MODEL(S), STYLIST, MAKE UP ARTIST, HAIRDRESSER, ...

FASHION DESIGN
CLOTHES, JEWELRY, SHOES...

DECORATION
FLOWERS, FURNITURE, ACCESSORIES, ...

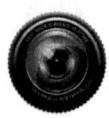

Shooting Sheet n°15

MY INSPIRATIONS

MY MOODBOARD

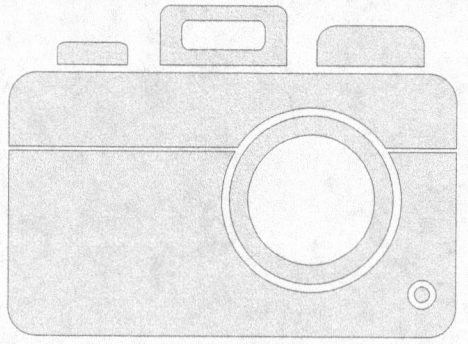

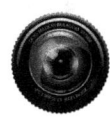

Shooting Sheet n°15

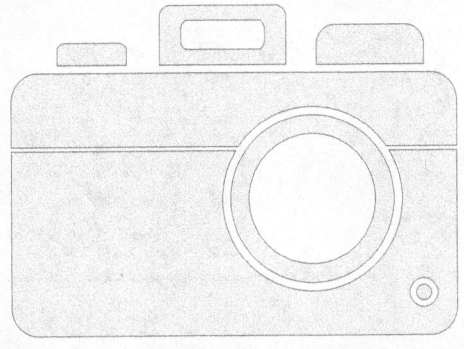

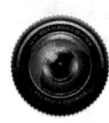

Shooting Sheet n°15

PHOTO SHOOTING

TECHNICAL SETTINGS

EQUIPMENT

PHOTO EDITING

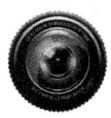

Shooting Sheet n°15

LIST OF SCENES & PLANS

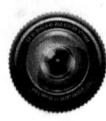

Shooting Sheet n°15

PUBLICATIONS

Notes

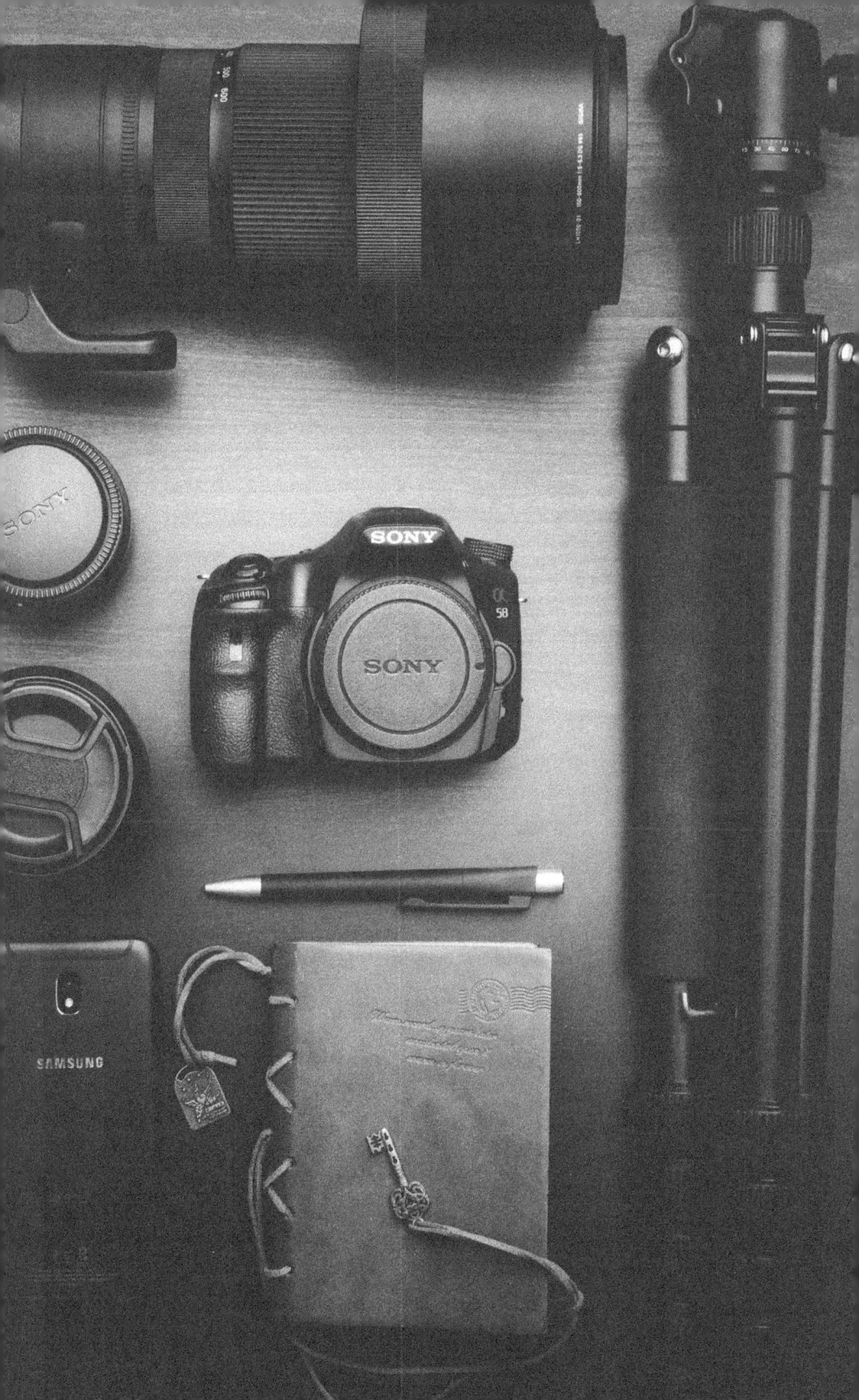

Notes

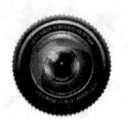

Notes

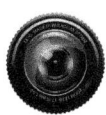

Notes

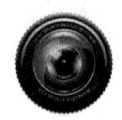

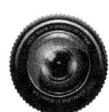

Notes

Notes

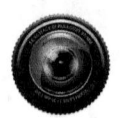

Notes

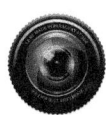

Notes

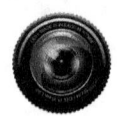

Notes

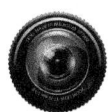

Notes

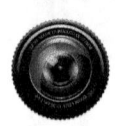

Notes

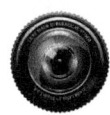

www.ingramcontent.com/pod-product-compliance
Lightning Source LLC
Chambersburg PA
CBHW070548220526
45467CB00003B/1123